SNAPSHOT

Milan & the Italian Lakes District

CONTENTS

INTRODUCTION

This Snapshot guide, excerpted from my guidebook *Rick Steves Italy*, introduces you to Milan. If Florence represents the Renaissance and Rome equals antiquity, Milan is 21st-century Italy. You can walk on the rooftop of one of Europe's grandest Gothic cathedrals, window-shop in fashionable neighborhoods, visit the world's most famous opera house, and admire a Leonardo masterpiece. Explore the city's grand, glass-domed arcade and stroll along one of Europe's longest pedestrian-only boulevards. Sip an *aperitivo* at a sidewalk café, and sample Milan's culinary specialties. If you're looking for a sophisticated, smart slice of Italy, you'll find it here.

I also cover the seductively beautiful Italian Lakes District. This region, where Italy meets the Alps, seems heaven-sent for nature lovers. Lake Como offers a mix of accessibility, scenery, and offbeatness with a heady whiff of 19th-century whimsy. Lake Maggiore, though more densely populated and more developed, has exotic garden islands and nearby mountains. The lakes are the place to take a vacation from your vacation, lingering in charming towns such as Varenna or Bellagio. Hop on a lake ferry and glide to dreamy villas, or ride a cable car to pristine alpine meadows.

To help you have the best trip possible, I've included the following topics in this book:

• **Planning Your Time**, with advice on how to make the most of your limited time

• **Orientation,** including tourist information (abbreviated as TI), tips on public transportation, local tour options, and helpful hints

• **Sights** with ratings:

▲▲▲—Don't miss

▲▲—Try hard to see
▲—Worthwhile if you can make it
No rating—Worth knowing about

• **Sleeping** and **Eating**, with good-value recommendations in every price range

• **Connections**, with tips on trains, buses, and driving

Practicalities, near the end of this book, has information on money, staying connected, hotel reservations, transportation, and more, plus Italian survival phrases.

To travel smartly, read this little book in its entirety before you go. It's my hope that this guide will make your trip more meaningful and rewarding. Traveling like a temporary local, you'll get the absolute most out of every mile, minute, and dollar.

Buon viaggio!

Rick Steves

MILAN

Milano

For every church in Rome, there's a bank in Milan. Italy's second city and the capital of the Lombardy region, Milan is a hardworking, fashion-conscious, time-is-money city of 1.3 million. It's a melting pot of people and history. Milan's industriousness may come from the Teutonic blood of its original inhabitants, the Lombards, or from its years under Austrian rule. Milan is Italy's fashion, industrial, banking, TV, publishing, and convention capital. The economic success of postwar Italy can be attributed, in part, to this city of publicists and pasta power-lunches.

As if to make up for its rough, noisy big-city-ness, the Milanesi people are works of art. Milan is an international fashion capital with a refined taste. Window displays are gorgeous, cigarettes are chic, and even the cheese comes gift-wrapped. Yet thankfully, Milan is no more expensive for tourists than other Italian cities.

Three hundred years before Christ, the Romans called this place Mediolanum, or "the place in the middle." By the fourth century A.D., it was the capital of the western half of the Roman Empire. Emperor Constantine issued the Edict of Milan from here, legalizing Christianity. After some barbarian darkness, medieval Milan became a successful mercantile city, eventually rising to regional prominence under the Visconti and Sforza families. By the time of the Renaissance, it was nicknamed "the New Athens," and was enough of a cultural center for Leonardo da Vinci to call it home. Then came 400 years of foreign domination (Spain, Austria, France, more Austria). Milan was a center of the 1848 revolution against Austria, and helped lead Italy to unification in 1870.

Mussolini left a heavy fascist touch on the architecture here

Milan

To Malpensa Airport,
Varenna, Stresa, Venice, etc.

CENTRAL
STATION

Monumental
Cemetery

PORTA
GARIBALDI
STATION

PIRELLI
TOWER

Airport
Buses

Monumentale

V.A. DORIA

To Como &
Malpensa
Airport

CORSO SEMPIONE

VIA LIB. PASANI

VIA VITRUVIO

VIA LEGNANO

CORSO BUENOS AIRES

To Fiera
di Milano
Trade Fair

Lima

Repubblica

VIA TURATI

Parco
Sempione

Turati

Porta
Venezia

BRANCA
TOWER

LAST
SUPPER
S. MARIA
D. GRAZIE

SFORZA
CASTLE

BRERA ART
GALLERY

Monte-
napoleone

CADORNA
STN.

VIA MONTE NAPOLEONE

Conc.

Cadorna

LA SCALA

RING
ROAD

To #16

C. MAGENTA

VIA MERAVIGLI

VIA DANTE

GALLERIA

Leonardo's
Horse &
Meazza
Stadium

Sant'
Ambrogio

Duomo

DUOMO

CORSO
PORTA VITTORIA

DA VINCI
NATIONAL SCIENCE
MUSEUM

Missori

VELASCO
TOWER

VIA TORINO

See Milan Hotels & Restaurants map

See Milan map

PORTO
TICINESE

PORTA
GENOVA
STATION

VIC.
LAY.

CORSO PORTA ROMANA

VIALE CALDARA

CORSO TICINESE

CORSO ITALIA

VIA CASALE

VIALE

Porta
Romana

VIA
FUSETTI

B. D'ESTE

RIPA DI PORTA TICINESE

NAVIGLI
DISTRICT

MAGOLFA

Naviglio Grande
Canal

1 Kilometer

1 Mile

(such as the central train station). His excesses also led to the WWII bombing of Milan. But the city rose again. The 1959 Pirelli Tower (the skinny skyscraper in front of the station) was a trendsetter in its day. Today, Milan is people-friendly, with a great transit system and inviting pedestrian zones.

Many tourists come to Italy for the past. But Milan is today's Italy. While it's not big on the tourist circuit, the city has plenty to see. And seeing Milan is not difficult: People-watchers and pigeon feeders could spend their entire visit never losing sight of the Duomo.

For pleasant excursions from the city, consider visiting Lake Como or Lake Maggiore—both are about an hour from Milan by train.

MILAN

PLANNING YOUR TIME

OK, it's a big, intense city, so you may not want to linger. Milan can't compare with Rome and Florence when it comes to art, but the city does have several unique and noteworthy sights: the Duomo and the Galleria Vittorio Emanuele II arcade, La Scala Opera House, Michelangelo's last *pietà* sculpture in Sforza Castle, and Leonardo's *Last Supper*.

With two nights and a full day, you can gain an appreciation for the town and see the major sights. On a short visit, I'd focus on the center. Tour the Duomo, hit any art you like (reserve ahead if you want to see *The Last Supper*), browse elegant shops and the Galleria Vittorio Emanuele II, and try to see an opera. To maximize your time in Milan, use the Metro to get around.

For those with a round-trip flight into Milan: The city is a cold plunge into the Italian deep end, so save it for the end of your trip and start your journey softly by going first to Lake Como (one-hour ride to Varenna) or the Cinque Terre (3-4 hours to Monterosso). Then spend the last night or two of your trip in Milan before flying home.

Monday is a terrible sightseeing day, since many museums are closed (including *The Last Supper*). August is oppressively hot and muggy, and locals who can vacate at this time do, leaving the city quiet. Those visiting in August find that the nightlife is sleepy, and many shops and restaurants are closed.

A Three-Hour Tour: If you're just changing trains at Milan's Centrale station (as, sooner or later, you probably will), consider catching a later train and taking this blitz tour: Check your bag at the station, ride the subway to the Duomo, peruse the square, explore the cathedral's rooftop and interior, drop into the Duomo Museum, have a scenic coffee in the Galleria Vittorio Emanuele II, spin on the floor mosaic of the bull for good luck, and maybe see a museum or two (most are within a 10-minute walk of the main square), and return by subway to the station. Art fans could make time for *The Last Supper* (if they've made reservations) and/or the Michelangelo *pietà* in Sforza Castle (no reservations necessary).

Orientation to Milan

My coverage focuses on the old center. Most sights and hotels listed are within a 15-minute walk of the cathedral (Duomo), which is a straight eight-minute Metro ride from the Centrale train station.

TOURIST INFORMATION

Milan's TI, at the La Scala end of the Galleria Vittorio Emanuele II, isn't worth a special trip (daily 9:00-19:00, Metro: Duomo, tel. 02-884-5555, www.turismo.milano.it).

ARRIVAL IN MILAN

Most visitors disembark at one of three major train stations: Milano Centrale, Porta Garibaldi, or Cadorna. Most Trenitalia trains, as well as airport buses and some airport trains, stop at Milano Centrale. Porta Garibaldi receives trains from France, some Trenitalia trains, and Italo trains from elsewhere in Italy. And Cadorna is the main terminus for trains from Malpensa Airport.

At Milano Centrale: The huge, sternly decorated, fascist-built (in 1931) central train station is a sight in itself. Recently cleaned, the halls feel more monumental than ever. Notice how the art makes you feel small—it emphasizes that a powerful state is a good thing. In the front lobby, heroic people celebrate "modern" transportation (circa-1930 ships, trains, and cars) opposite reliefs depicting old-fashioned sailboats and horse carts.

Moving walkways link the station's three main levels: platforms on top, shops on a small mezzanine, and most services at ground level (pay WCs and ATMs are abundant). For baggage check *(deposito bagagli)*, taxis, or buses to the airports, turn right at ground level toward the exit marked *Piazza Luigi di Savoia*. Just outside the station's front entrance are car-rental offices, the Metro, and escalators down to a fourth basement level with a few shops. (You can also enter the Metro directly from inside the station—just follow signs.)

"Centrale" is a misnomer—the Duomo is a 35-minute walk away. But it's a straight shot on the Metro (8 minutes). Buy a €1.50 ticket at a kiosk or from the machines, follow signs for yellow line 3 (direction: San Donato), go four stops to the Duomo stop, surface, and you'll be facing the cathedral.

To **buy train tickets,** use the Trenitalia machines for most domestic trips (Trenord machines by track 3 sell commuter-rail tickets for Malpensa Airport). For international tickets or complicated questions, join the line at the Trenitalia ticket office on the ground floor. Another alternative is the Agenzie 365 travel agency, a private company selling tickets at a 7 percent markup from various offices in the station (a reasonable price to pay to skip the Trenitalia ticket lines, but the agency often has a line of its own). The most convenient office is just inside the Piazza Luigi di Savoia.

At Milano Cadorna: You're most likely to use this commuter railway station if you take the Malpensa Express airport train, which uses track 1. The Cadorna Metro station—with a direct connection to the Duomo on Metro red line 1—is directly out front.

Rome vs. Milan: A Classic Squabble

In Italy, the North and South bicker about each other, hurling barbs, quips, and generalizations. All the classic North/South traits can be applied to Milan (the business capital) and Rome (the government and religious capital). People like to say that people come to Milan to sin, and they go to Rome to ask for forgiveness.

The Milanesi say the Romans are lazy. Government jobs in Rome come with short hours—

made even shorter by multiple coffee breaks, three-hour lunches, chats with colleagues, and phone calls to friends and relatives. Milanesi contend that "Roma *ladrona*" (Rome, the big thief) is a parasite that lives off the taxes of people up North. There's still a strong Milan-based movement promoting secession from the South.

Romans, meanwhile, dismiss the Milanesi as uptight workaholics with nothing else to live for—gray like their foggy city. Romans do admit that in Milan, job opportunities are better and based on merit. And the Milanesi grudgingly concede the Romans have a gift for enjoying life.

While Rome is more of a family city, Milan is the place for

At Milano Porta Garibaldi: Italo trains, with high-speed service to Florence, Rome, and Naples, use Porta Garibaldi Station, north of the city center, as do some Trenitalia trains and the high-speed TGV from Paris. Porta Garibaldi is on Metro green line 2, two stops from Milano Centrale.

By Car: Leonardo never drove in Milan. Smart guy. Driving here is bad enough to make the €30/day fee for a downtown garage a blessing. If you're driving, do Milan (and Lake Como) before or after you rent your car, not while you've got it. If you must have a car, use the safe, affordable, well-marked park-and-ride lots at suburban Metro stations such as Cascina Gobba. These are shown on the official Metro map, and full details are at www.atm.it (click on English, then "Car Parks," then "Parking Lots").

By Plane: See "Milan Connections" at the end of this chapter.

HELPFUL HINTS

Theft Alert: Be on guard. Milan's thieves target tourists, especially at the Centrale train station, getting in and out of the subway, and around the Duomo. They can be dressed as tourists, high-powered singles on the career fast-track. Milanese yuppies mix with each other...not the city's longtime residents. Milan is seen as wary of foreigners and inward-looking, and Rome as fun-loving, tolerant, and friendly. In Milan, bureaucracy (like social

services) works logically and efficiently, while in Rome, accomplishing even small chores can be exasperating. Everything in Rome—from finding a babysitter to buying a car—is done through friends.

Milanesi find Romans vulgar. The Roman dialect is considered one of the coarsest in the country. Much as they try, Milanesi just can't say "Damn your dead relatives" quite as effectively as the Romans. Still, Milanesi enjoy Roman comedians and love to imitate the accent.

The Milanesi feel that Rome is dirty and Roman traffic nerve-wracking. But despite the craziness, Rome maintains a genuine village feel. People share family news with their neighborhood grocer. Milan lacks people-friendly piazzas, and entertainment comes at a high price. But in Rome, *la dolce vita* is as close as the nearest square, and a full moon is enjoyed by all.

businessmen, or beggars, or they can be gangs of too-young-to-arrest children. Watch out for ragged people carrying newspaper and cardboard—they'll thrust this item at you as a distraction while they pick your pocket. If you're ripped off and plan to file an insurance claim, fill out a report with the police (Police Station, "Questura," Via Fatebenefratelli 11, Metro: Turati, open daily 24 hours, tel. 02-62261).

Medical Help: Dial 118 for medical emergencies. There are two medical clinics with emergency care facilities (both closed Sat-Sun): the **International Health Center** in Galleria Strasburgo (between Via Durini and Corso Europa, at #3, third floor, Metro: San Babila, tel. 02-7634-0720, www.ihc.it) and the **American International Medical Center** at Via Mercalli 11 (Metro: Missori or Crocetta, call for appointment, tel. 02-5831-9808, www.aimclinic.it).

Bookstores: The handiest major bookstore is **La Feltrinelli,** under the Galleria Vittorio Emanuele II (daily, tel. 02-8699-6903). The **American Bookstore** is at Via Manfredo Camperio 16, near Sforza Castle (closed Sun, Metro: Cairoli, tel. 02-878-920).

Laundry: Allwash, at Via Savona 2, just off Via Zugna, is the closest launderette to the center. Take tram #14 (direction: Cim. Maggiore-Lorenteggio) to Piazzale Cantore, or go by Metro to Porta Genova and walk 5-10 minutes (daily 8:00-22:00, English instructions, tel. 800-030-653, www.allwash.it).

Soccer: For a dose of Europe's soccer mania (which many believe provides a necessary testosterone vent to keep Europe out of a third big war), catch a match while you're here. A.C. Milan and Inter Milan are the ferociously competitive home teams (tickets-€10-350, www.acmilan.com or www.inter.it, bring your passport to the game for security reasons). Both teams play in the 85,000-seat Meazza Stadium (a.k.a. San Siro) most Sunday afternoons from September to June (ride the Metro purple line 5 to San Siro Stadio).

GETTING AROUND MILAN

By Public Transit: It's a pleasure to use Milan's great public transit system, called ATM ("ATM Point" info desk in Duomo Metro station, www.atm.it). The clean, spacious, fast, and easy **Metro** zips you nearly anywhere you may want to go, and trams and city buses fill in the gaps. The handiest Metro line for a quick visit is the yellow line 3, which connects the Centrale train station to the Duomo. The other lines are red (1), green (2), and purple (5). A new line 4 will eventually connect San Babila and Linate Airport (possibly in 2016). The Metro shuts down about half past midnight, but many trams continue until 1:00 or even 2:00.

A **single ticket,** valid for 90 minutes, can be used for one ride, including transfers, on all forms of transport (€1.50; sold at newsstands, tobacco shops, shops with *ATM* sticker in window, and at machines in subway stations). Other ticket options include a *carnet* (€13.80 for 10 rides—it's one magnetic ticket that can be validated 10 times); a **24-hour pass** (€4.50, worthwhile if you take at least four rides); and a **48-hour pass** (€8.25, pays off with six rides). Tickets must be run through the machines at Metro turnstiles and at the front and rear of trams—also each time you transfer.

By Taxi: Small groups go cheap and fast by taxi (drop charge-€3.30, €1.10/kilometer; €5.40 drop charge on Sun and holidays, €6.50 from 21:00 to 6:00 in the morning). It can be easier to walk to a taxi stand than to flag down a cab. Handy stands are at Piazza del Duomo and in front of Sforza Castle (tel. 02-8585 or 02-6969).

By Bike: Like many big cities in Europe, Milan has a public bike system, **BikeMi.** You can set up a temporary subscription (€6/week or €2.50/day) online or at an "ATM Point" public transit info office (a handy one is in the Duomo Metro station). You'll receive a user code and password, allowing you to pick up a bike at any Bike-Mi station, generally located near Metro stations. Enter your code and password on the keypad, grab the assigned bike, and you're on your way (first 30 minutes free, then €0.50/each 30 minutes up to 2 hours, then €2/hour, www.bikemi.com).

Tours in Milan

Local Guides
Lorenza Scorti is a hardworking young guide who knows her city's history and how to teach it (€150/3 hours, €300/6 hours, same price for individuals or groups, evenings OK, mobile 347-735-1346, lorenza.scorti@libero.it). **Sara Cerri** is another good licensed local guide who enjoys teaching (€190/3 hours, then €50/hour, mobile

MILAN

Central Milan

Piazza Sempione

ARENA

VIA LEGNANO

To Malpensa Airport & Como

BRANCA TOWER

Parco Sempione

See Milan Hotels & Restaurants detail map

VIALE MOLIERE

TRIENNALE DI MILANO

PALAZZO DELL'ARTE

VIA GADIO

FORO

Lanza M

BUONAPARTE

To Fiera di Milano Trade Fair

V. 20 SETTEMBRE

VIA VICENZO MONTI

SFORZA CASTLE

ENTRANCE TO MUSEUM OF ANCIENT ART

Piazza Castello

MICHELANGELO'S PIETÀ

ZANI VIAGGI TOURS

FORO

AUTOSTRADALE TOUR OFFICE

Largo Cairoli

Cairoli M

CADORNA STATION

M Cadorna

BUONAPARTE

VIA GIOVANNI BOCCACCIO

SCHOKOLAT

TEATRO DAL VERME

AMERICAN BOOKSTORE

VIA G. PUCCINI

VIA CARADOSSO

LAST SUPPER

S. MARIA D. GRAZIE

ANTICA LOCANDA LEONARDO

T #16

CORSO MAGENTA

To Leonardo's Horse & Meazza Stadium

PALAZZO DELLE STELLINE

V. CARDUCCI

PALAZZO LITTA

CORSO T #16 MAGENTA

VIA G. PUCCINI

S. GIOVANNI MURO

V. CAMPERIO

VIA MERAVIGLI

BORSA

Piazza degli Affari

SAN MAURIZIO

ARCHAEOLOGICAL MUSEUM

VIA LUINI

BRISA

THE FINGER

VIA S. BORROMEI

V. SANT' AGNESE

VIA GIOSUÈ CARDUCCI

V. SANT NIRONE

VIA

OSPEDALE S. GIUSEPPE

VIA SAN VITTORE

B&B HOTEL MILANO SANT'AMBROGIO

S. VITTORE AL CORPO

DA VINCI NATIONAL SCIENCE MUSEUM

VIA TERRAGGIO

BASILICA DI S. AMBROGIO

V. L. NECCHI

UNIVERSITÀ CATTOLICA

VIA SANT'ORSOLA

VIA SANTA MARTA

VIA CAPPUCCIO

M Sant' Ambrogio

PUSTERLA DI S. AMBROGIO

VIA LANZONE

VIA OLONA

V. CAM

VIA AUSONIO

EDMONDO DE AMICIS

VIA CORENTI

VIA STAMPA

VIA SAN VITO

VIA MORA

M Sant'Agostino

VIA ARIBERTO

S. VINCENZO

VIA G. DA SESTO

VIA CALOGERO

CORSO GENOVA

S. LORENZO

VIALE PAPINIANO

V. CON ZUGNA

V. SIMONETTA

To Navigli District

V. MOLINO D. ARMI

380-433-3019, www.walkingtourmilan.it, walkingtourmilan@ gmail.com). **Ludovic Charles Goudin** is energetic and has a passion for teaching art (€180/3 hours, mobile 331-289-3464, ludovicgoudin@yahoo.it).

Walking and Bus Tours with *The Last Supper*

If your visit to Milan is fast approaching and you can't get a reservation for *The Last Supper,* consider joining a walking or bus tour that includes a guided visit to Leonardo's masterpiece. These €60-75 tours (usually three hours) also take you to top sights such as the Duomo, Galleria Vittorio Emanuele II, La Scala Opera House, and Sforza Castle. Ideally book the tour several days in advance, but it's worth a try at the last minute, too.

For the best experience, I'd book a walking tour with **Veditalia** (www.veditalia.com) or **City Wonders** (www.citywonders.com). Both have good guides and solid reputations. The bus-and-walking tours are less satisfying, but you can try **Autostradale** ("Look Mi" tour, offices in passage at far end of Piazza del Duomo and in front of Sforza Castle, tel. 02-8058-1354, www.autostradale.it) or **Zani Viaggi** (office disguised as a "tourist information" point on the square facing Sforza Castle at Foro Bonaparte 76, tel. 02-867-131, www.zaniviaggi.it).

Hop-On, Hop-Off Option: Zani Viaggi also operates the **CitySightseeing Milano** hop-on, hop-off buses (look for the red buses—easiest at Duomo and La Scala, €22/all day, €25/48 hours, buy on board, recorded commentary, www.milano.city-sightseeing. it). With a bus ticket, you can pay an additional €33 for a *Last Supper* reservation—an exorbitant price, but worth considering for the wealthy and the desperate.

Sights in Milan

▲▲DUOMO (CATHEDRAL)

The city's centerpiece is the fourth-largest church in Europe (after the Vatican's, London's, and Sevilla's). At 525 by 300 feet, the place

is immense, with more than two thousand statues inside (and another thousand outside) and 52 one-hundred-foot-tall, sequoia-size pillars representing the weeks of the year and the liturgical calendar. If you do two laps, you've done your daily walk. It was built to hold

40,000 worshippers, the entire population of Milan when construction began. A visit here has three parts: the church interior; the adjacent Duomo Museum; and an elevator ride (or long climb) up to the rooftop for a stroll through its forest of jagged spires.

Cost and Hours: Church—€2, daily 7:00-19:00; Duomo Museum—€6, Tue-Sun 10:00-18:00, closed Mon; roof terraces—by elevator-€13, via stairs-€8, daily 9:00-19:00, last ascent at 18:00. If you're doing all three sights—which I recommend—ask about a combo-ticket, which will likely save you plenty.

Information: Directly behind the Duomo is the uncrowded **Duomo Info Point** office, which can be a good place to buy your ticket (Mon-Sat 9:30-17:30, Sun 11:00-15:00). Church tel. 02-7202-2656, museum tel. tel. 02-860-358, www.duomomilano.it.

Dress Code: Modest dress is required to visit the church. Don't wear shorts or anything sleeveless—even children.

Tours: A €6 audioguide for the church is available at a kiosk inside the main door of the church (no rentals Sun, 1.5 hours).

Background

Back when Europe was fragmented into countless tiny kingdoms and dukedoms, the dukes of Milan wanted to impress their counterparts in Germany and France. Their goal was to earn Milan recognition and respect from both the Vatican and the kings and princes of northern Europe by building a massive, richly ornamented cathedral. Even after Renaissance-style domes had come into vogue elsewhere in Italy, conservative Milan stuck with the Gothic style. The dukes thought northerners would relate better to Gothic, and they loaded the cathedral with pointed arches and spires. For good measure, the cathedral was built not from ordinary stone, but from marble, top to bottom. Pink Candoglia marble was rafted in from a quarry about 60 miles away, across Lake Maggiore and down a canal to a port at the cathedral. Construction lasted from 1386 to 1810, with final touches added as late as 1965. In 2014, archaeologists probing for ancient Roman ruins beneath the Duomo discovered the remains of what might be a temple to the goddess Minerva.

○ Self-Guided Duomo Tour

Begin by looping around the Duomo's exterior, then head inside to enjoy its remarkable bulk, fine stained-glass windows, and Baroque altar.

Exterior

Walk around the entire church exterior and notice the statues, made between the 14th and 20th centuries by sculptors from all over Europe. There are hundreds of them—each different and quite

Milan at a Glance

▲▲**Duomo** Milan's showpiece cathedral, with an amazing roof you can walk on. **Hours:** Church—daily 7:00-19:00, rooftop terraces—daily 9:00-19:00, last ascent at 18:00. See page 12.

▲▲**Galleria Vittorio Emanuele II** Glass-domed arcade on the main square, perfect for window-shopping and people-watching. **Hours:** Always open. See page 21.

▲▲**La Scala Opera House and Museum** The world's most prestigious opera house. **Hours:** Museum daily 9:00-12:30 & 13:30-17:30. See page 24.

▲▲**Basilica di Sant'Ambrogio** Historic, art-packed church dating to early Roman times. **Hours:** Mon-Sat 10:00-12:30 & 14:30-18:30, Sun 15:00-18:00. See page 29.

▲▲*The Last Supper* Leonardo da Vinci's masterpiece, displayed in the Church of Santa Maria delle Grazie (viewable only with a reservation). **Hours:** Tue-Sun 8:15-18:45 (last entry), closed Mon. See page 31.

▲**Duomo Museum** Church art and original sculptures from Milan's cathedral. **Hours:** Tue-Sun 10:00-18:00, closed Mon. See page 19.

▲**Piazza del Duomo** Milan's main square, full of energy, history, and pickpockets. **Hours:** Always open. See page 21.

▲**Museo del Novecento** Milan's 20th-century art collection, housed in the fascist-era City Hall. **Hours:** Mon 14:30-19:30, Tue-Wed, Fri, and Sun 9:30-19:30, Thu and Sat 9:30-22:30. See page 22.

▲**Piazza dei Mercanti** The evocative medieval heart of the city. **Hours:** Always open. See page 23.

▲**Gallerie d'Italia** Three adjacent palaces filled with 19th- and 20th-century Italian art. **Hours:** Tue-Sun 9:30-19:30, Thu until 22:30, closed Mon. See page 25.

▲**Pinacoteca Ambrosiana** Oldest museum in Milan, with works by Raphael, Leonardo, Botticelli, Titian, and Caravaggio. **Hours:** Tue-Sun 10:00-18:00, closed Mon. See page 26.

▲**Church of San Maurizio** The "Sistine Chapel of Lombardy," gorgeously frescoed by Bernardino Luini, a follower of Leonardo. **Hours:** Tue-Sat 9:30-17:30, Sun 13:30-17:30, closed Mon. See page 28.

▲**Leonardo da Vinci National Science and Technology Museum** Leonardo's designs illustrated in wooden models, plus a vast collection of historical and technological bric-a-brac and machines. **Hours:** Tue-Fri and Sun 9:30-17:00, Sat 9:30-18:30, closed Mon. See page 30.

▲▲**Brera Art Gallery** World-class collection of Italian paintings (13th-20th century), including Raphael, Caravaggio, Gentile da Fabriano, Piero della Francesca, Mantegna, and the Bellini brothers. **Hours:** Tue-Sun 8:30-19:15, closed Mon. See page 33.

▲▲**Sforza Castle** Milan's castle, whose highlight is an unfinished Michelangelo *pietà*. **Hours:** Tue-Sun 9:00-17:30, closed Mon. See page 35.

▲**Via Dante** Human traffic frolics to lilting accordions on one of Europe's longest pedestrian-only boulevards. **Hours:** Always open. See page 38.

▲**Naviglio Grande** Milan's old canal port—once a working-class zone, now an atmospheric nightspot for dinner or drinks. **Hours:** Always open. See page 38.

▲**Monumental Cemetery** Evocative final resting spot with tombs showcasing expressive art styles from 1870 to 1930. **Hours:** Tue-Sun 8:00-18:00, closed Mon. See page 39.

Poldi Pezzoli Museum Italian paintings (15th-18th century), weaponry, and decorative arts. **Hours:** Wed-Mon 10:00-18:00, closed Tue. See page 35.

Bagatti Valsecchi Museum 19th-century Italian Renaissance furnishings. **Hours:** Tue-Sun 13:00-17:45, closed Mon. See page 35.

Leonardo's Horse Gargantuan equestrian monument built from Leonardo's designs. **Hours:** Always viewable. See page 39.

MILAN

creative. Look at the statues on the tips of the many spires...they seem so relaxed, like they're just hanging out, waiting for their big day. Functioning as drain spouts, the 96 fanciful gargoyle monsters are especially imaginative.

As you stand outside at the back of the church (near the Duomo Info Point), imagine the glory of this first wall. These were the earliest stones, laid at the end of the 14th century. The sun-in-rose window was the proud symbol of the city's leading Visconti family; it's flanked by the angel telling Mary she's going to bear the Messiah. And to your right is a shrine to the leading religion of the 21st century: soccer. The Football Team store is filled with colorful vestments and relics of local soccer saints.

Continue circling the cathedral. Back at the front, enjoy the statues enlivening the facade. The lower ones—full of energy and movement—are early Baroque, from about 1600. Of the five doors, the center one is biggest. Made in 1907 in the Liberty Style (Italian Art Nouveau), it features the Joy and Sorrow of the Virgin Mary. Sad scenes are on the left, joyful ones on the right, and on top is the coronation of Mary in heaven by Jesus, with all the saints and angels looking on. Step up close and study the fine reliefs.

Interior

Enter the church. Stand at the back of the fourth-longest nave in Christendom. The apse at the far end was started in 1385. The

wall behind you wasn't finished until 1520. Even though the Renaissance had begun, builders stuck with the Gothic style. The two single-stone marble pillars flanking the main door are the most precious ones in the church.

Notice two tiny lights: The little red one on the cross above the altar marks where a nail from the cross of Jesus is kept. This relic was brought to Milan by St. Helen (Emperor Constantine's mother) in the fourth century, when Milan was the capital of the western Roman Empire. It's on display for three days a year (in mid-Sept). Now look high to the right, in the rear corner of the church, and find a tiny pinhole of white light. This is designed to shine a 10-inch sunbeam at noon onto the bronze line that runs across the floor, indicating where we are on the zodiac (but local guides claim they've never seen it work).

• *Wander deeper into the church, up the right aisle. Check out the...*

Stained-Glass Windows: The brilliant and expensive colored glass (stained, not painted) is from the 15th century. Bought by wealthy families seeking the Church's favor, the windows face south to get the most light. The altars below generally honor the patron who made each window possible. Pick out familiar scenes in the windows, whose purpose was to teach the illiterate masses the way to salvation through stories from the Old Testament and the life of Jesus. On the opposite wall (left side), many of the windows are more modern—from the 16th to the 20th century—and are either made of dimmer, cheaper painted glass or are replacements for ones destroyed by the concussion of WWII bombs that fell nearby.

There are a couple of stops of interest along the right aisle. Under the third window, you can trace the uninterrupted rule of 144 local archbishops back to A.D. 51.

The fifth window dates from 1470, "just" 85 years after the first stone of the cathedral was laid. The window shows the story of Jesus, from Annunciation to Crucifixion. In the bottom window, as the angel Gabriel tells Mary the news, the Holy Spirit (in the form of a dove) enters Mary's window and world. Compare the exquisite beauty of this window to the cruder 19th-century window on the right.

The seventh window is modern, from the 1980s. Bright and bold, it celebrates two local cardinals (whose tombs and bodies are behind glass). This memorial to Cardinal Ferrari and Cardinal Schuster, who heroically helped the Milanese out of their post-WWII blues, is a reminder that this great church is more than a tourist attraction—it's a living part of Milan.

• *Now face the...*

Main Altar: While the church is Gothic, the area around the altar is Baroque—a dramatic stage-like setting in the style of the Vatican in the 1570s (a Roman-Catholic statement to counter the mostly Gothic Protestant churches of the north). Napoleon crowned himself King of Italy under this dome in 1805. Now look to the rear, up at the ceiling, and see the fancy "carving" (between the ribs)—nope, that's painted. It looks expensive, but paint is more affordable than carved stone.

• *In the south (right) transept, find the bald statue lit by the open door.*

St. Bartolomeo Statue: This is a grotesque 16th-century statue of St. Bartolomeo, an apostle and first-century martyr skinned alive by the Romans. Examine the details (face, hands, feet) of the poor guy wearing his own skin like a robe. Carved by a student of Leonardo da Vinci, this is a study in human anatomy learned by dissection, forbidden by the Church at the time.

• *As you walk around the interior, look down at the fine 16th-century inlaid-marble...*

Floor: The pieces around the altar are original. You can tell that the black marble (quarried from Lake Como) is harder because it looks and feels less worn than the other colors (white from Lake Maggiore, pink from Verona).

• *Walk toward the altar, then bear right around the corner 30 steps. You'll see a door marked* Scurolo di S. Carlo. *This leads down to the...*

Crypt of St. Charles Borromeo: Steps lead under the altar to the tombs of St. Charles Borromeo (1538-1584, the economic power behind the church) and his family. You can still see Charles' withered body in the glass case. Charles was bishop of Milan, and the second most important hometown saint after St. Ambrose. Tarnished silver reliefs around the ceiling show scenes from Charles' life.

• *Now continue around the apse, looking up at the...*

Windows: The apse is lit by three huge windows, all 19th-century painted copies. The originals, destroyed in Napoleonic times, were made of precious stained glass.

• *Circling around to the far side, head all the way up the aisle. Before you leave, directly to the right of the main door, notice the entrance and stairs down, marked* Archaeological Area. *This takes you down to the...*

Paleo-Christian Baptistery of San Giovanni: In the rear of the church, you can climb down into the church that stood here long before the present one. Milan was an important center of early Christianity. In Roman times, Mediolanum's streets were 10 feet below today's level. You'll see the scant remains of an eight-sided baptistery (where Sts. Augustine and Ambrose were baptized) and a little church. Back then, since you couldn't enter the church until you were baptized (which didn't happen until age 18), churches had a little "holy zone" just outside for the unbaptized. This included a baptistery like this one.

More Duomo Sights
▲▲Duomo Rooftop

Strolling between the frilly spires of the cathedral rooftop is the most memorable part of a Duomo visit. You can climb the stairs

or take the elevator (for specifics, see "Cost and Hours," earlier). Both entrances are around the left side of the church: the stairs are in front of the transept, and the elevator is behind it. (Even those taking the elevator will also have to climb some stairs.)

Once up there, you'll do a one-way loop around the rooftop, wandering through a fancy forest of spires with great views of the city, the square, and—on clear days—the crisp and jagged Alps to the north. And, 330 feet above everything, La

Madonnina overlooks it all. This 15-foot-tall gilded Virgin Mary is a symbol of the city.

▲Duomo Museum (Museo del Duomo)

This museum, across from the Duomo in the Palazzo Reale, helps fill in the rest of the story of Milan's cathedral, and lets you see its original art and treasures up close (for specifics, see "Cost and Hours," earlier). The collection lacks description (in any language) and is virtually meaningless without an audioguide (€5). It's worth a walk-through if you buy the combo-ticket and have an interest in old church art.

Visiting the Museum: Just after the ticket taker, notice (on the wall to your right) the original **inlaid-marble floor** of the Duomo. The black (from Lake Como) marble is harder. Go ahead, wear down the white a little more.

Now follow the one-way route. Among the early treasures of the cathedral is a 900-year-old, Byzantine-style **crucifix.** Made of copper gilded with real gold and nailed onto wood, it hung in the church that stood here previously, as well as in today's cathedral.

You'll pass a big, wooden model of the church (we'll get a better look at this later, on the way out). Then you'll step through a long room with paintings, chalices, glass monstrances, and lifelike reliquary busts of Sts. Charles, Sebastian, and Thecla.

Look for the big statue of **St. George.** Among the oldest cathedral statues, it once stood on the front spire and shows nearly 600 years of pollution and aging. Some think this is the face of Duke Visconti—the man who started the cathedral. The museum is filled with original statues and spires like this, carved of *marmo di Candoglia*—marble from Candoglia. The duke's family gave the entire Candoglia quarry (near Stresa) to the church for all the marble it would ever need.

You'll pop into a long room filled with more statues. On your left, gaze—as did pilgrims 500 years ago—into the eyes of **God the Father.** Made of wood, wrapped in copper, and gilded, this giant head covered the keystone connecting the tallest arches directly above the high altar of the Duomo.

Continue into a narrow room lined with grotesque **gargoyles.** When attached to the cathedral, they served two purposes: to scare away evil spirits and to spew rainwater away from the building.

Twist through several more rooms of statues big and small. In one long, brick-walled hall, watch on the left for **St. Paul the Hermit,** who got close to God by living in the desert. While wearing only a simple robe, he's filled with inner richness. The intent is for pilgrims to commune with him and feel at peace (but I couldn't stop thinking of the Cowardly Lion).

A few steps beyond Paul, look for the 15th-century dandy with the rolled-up contract in his hand. That's Visconti's descendant, Galeazzo Sforza, and if it weren't for him, the church facade might still be brick as bare as the walls of this room. The contract he holds makes it official—the church now owns the marble quarry (and it makes money on it to this day).

In the next room, study the brilliantly gilded, dynamic, full-bodied statue of *God the Father* (1554). Also keep an eye out for a sumptuous Flanders-style **tapestry,** woven of silk, silver, and gold. Half a millennium ago, this hung from the high altar. In true Flemish style, it weaves vivid details of everyday life into the theology. It tells the story of the Crucifixion by showing three scenes at once. Note the exquisite detail, down to the tears on Mary's cheeks.

Next you'll step through a stunning room with 360 degrees of gorgeous **stained glass** from the 12th to 15th century. Go ahead—take a close look at details that used to be too far above the cathedral floor to be seen clearly.

Soon you'll reach a display of **terra-cotta panels** juxtaposed with large **monochrome paintings** (1628) by Giovanni Battista Crespi. After Crespi finished the paintings, they were translated into terra-cotta, and finally sculpted in marble to decorate the doorways of the cathedral. Study Crespi's *Creation of Eve (Creazione di Eva)* and its terra-cotta twin. This served as the model for the marble statue that still stands above the center door on the church's west portal (1643). You'll pass a few more of these scenes, then hook into a room with the original, stone-carved, swirling *Dancing Angels*, which decorated the ceiling over the door.

After passing several big tapestries, and a huge warehouse where statues are stacked on shelves stretching up to the ceiling, you'll reach the ***Frame of the Madonnina*** (1773). Standing like a Picasso is the original iron frame for the statue of the Virgin Mary that still crowns the cathedral's tallest spire. In 1967, a steel replacement was made for the 33 pieces of gilded copper bolted to the frame. The carved-wood face of Mary (in the corner) is the original mold for Mary's cathedral-crowning copper face.

Soon you'll get a better look at that **wooden model** of the Duomo. This was the actual model—necessary in that pre-computer age—used in the 16th century by the architects and engineers to build the church. This version of the facade wasn't actually built; other rejected facades line the walls.

On your way out, you'll pass models for the Duomo's doors. And stepping outside, as your eyes adjust to the sunlight, you'll see the grand church itself—looking so glorious thanks to the many centuries of hard work you've just learned about.

AROUND THE DUOMO
▲Piazza del Duomo
Milan's main square is a classic European scene and a popular local gathering point. Professionals scurry, fashion-conscious kids loiter, and young thieves peruse.

Stand in the square midway between the statue and the Galleria. You're surrounded by history. The **statue** is Victor Emmanuel II, the first king of Italy. He's looking at the grand Galleria named for him. The words above the triumphal arch entrance read: "To Victor Emmanuel II, from the people of Milan."

Opposite the Galleria, flanking Via Marconi, are the twin fascist buildings of the Arengario Palace, which houses the **Museo del Novecento** (described later). Mussolini made grandiose speeches from their balconies. Study the buildings' relief panels, which tell—with fascist melodrama—the history of Milan.

To the left of these buildings is the historic ducal palace, **Palazzo Reale.** This building, now housing the Duomo Museum (described earlier) and temporary art exhibits, was redone in the Neoclassical style by Empress Maria Theresa in the late 1700s, when Milan was ruled by the Austrian Habsburgs.

Behind the Victor Emmanuel II statue (opposite the cathedral, about a block beyond the square), hiding in a small courtyard, is **Piazza dei Mercanti,** the center of medieval Milan (described later).

▲▲Galleria Vittorio Emanuele II
This breathtaking four-story glass-domed arcade, next to Piazza del Duomo, is a symbol of Milan. The iron-and-glass structure

(built during the age of Eiffel and the heady days of Italian unification) showcased a new, modern era. It was the first building in town to have electric lighting, and from its inception, has been an elegant and popular meeting place. (Sadly, its designer, Giuseppe Mengoni, died the day before the gallery opened.) Here you can turn an expensive cup of coffee into a good value by enjoying some of Europe's best people-watching.

The venerable **Bar Camparino** (at

the Galleria's Piazza del Duomo entry), with a friendly staff and a period interior, is the former haunt of famous opera composer Giuseppe Verdi and conductor Arturo Toscanini, who used to stop by after their performances at La Scala. It's a fine place to enjoy a drink and people-watch (€3.50 for an espresso is a great deal if you relax and enjoy the view, or €1 at the bar just to experience the scene). The café is named after the Campari family (its first owners), originators of the famous red Campari bitter (Tue-Sun 7:30-20:00, closed Mon and Aug, tel. 02-8646-4435).

Wander around the Galleria. Its art celebrates the establishment of Italy as an independent country. Around the central dome,

patriotic mosaics symbolize the four major continents (sorry, Australia). The mosaic floor is also patriotic. The white cross in the center represents the king. The she-wolf with Romulus and Remus (on the south side—facing Rome) honors the city that, since 1870, has been the national capital. On the west side (facing Torino, the provisional capital of Italy from 1861 to 1865), you'll find that city's symbol: a *torino* (little bull). For good luck, locals step on his irresistible little testicles. Two local girls explained to me that it works better if you spin—two times, and it must be clockwise. Find the poor little bull and observe for a few minutes...it's a cute scene. With so much spinning, the mosaic is replaced every few years.

Luxury shops have had outlets here from the beginning. Along with Gucci, Louis Vuitton, and Prada, you'll find Borsalino (at the end near Piazza della Scala), which has been selling hats here since the gallery opened in 1877.

If you cut through the Galleria to the other side, you'll pop out at Piazza della Scala, with its famous opera house and the Gallerie d'Italia (all described later).

▲Museo del Novecento

Milan's 20th-century art fills the two buildings of the Arengario Palace, Mussolini's fascist-era City Hall. In the beautifully laid-out museum, you'll work your way up the escalators and through the last century, one decade at a time. Each section is well-described in English, and the capper is a fine panoramic view over Piazza del Duomo through grand fascist-era arches.

Cost and Hours: €5; Mon 14:30-19:30; Tue-Wed, Fri, and

Sun 9:30-19:30; Thu and Sat 9:30-22:30; last admission one hour before closing, audioguide-€5, facing Piazza del Duomo at Via Marconi 1, tel. 02-8844-4072, www.museodelnovecento.org.

Visiting the Museum: As you spiral up the big ramp, the first painting you'll see, partway up, is Giuseppe Pellizza da Volpedo's *The Fourth Estate* (1901). It celebrates the humanistic, socialist spirit that came with the arrival of the 20th century, and prepares you for the spirit of the collection. The first rooms feature small pieces by big international names (Picasso, Braque, Matisse), but the stars of the show are Italian avant-garde artists such as Umberto Boccioni, a seminal Futurist whose abstract paintings and sculptures convey the dynamism of the modern age. From here, watch art styles evolve, from anything-goes modernism, to a lull of pretty landscapes between the world wars, to the rigid rise of fascist art. Other highlights include sculptures from the 1930s by Arturo Martini and Fausto Melotti. Finally, you'll arrive nearly at the present day, with abstraction, contemporary installations, and kinetic (moving) art, as well as a special exhibit on Marino Marini, an influential mid-20th-century sculptor.

▲Piazza dei Mercanti

This small square, the center of political power in 13th-century Milan, hides one block off Piazza del Duomo (directly opposite

the cathedral). A strangely peaceful place today, it offers a fine smattering of historic architecture that escaped the bombs of World War II.

The arcaded, red-brick building that dominates the square was the City Hall (Palazzo della Ragione); its arcades once housed the market hall. Overlooking the wellhead in the middle of the square is a balcony with a coats of arms—this is where new laws were announced. Eventually two big families—Visconti and Sforza—took power, Medici-style, in Milan; the snake is their symbol. Running the show in Renaissance times, these dynasties shaped much of the city we see today, including the Duomo and the fortress. In 1454, the Sforza family made peace with Venice while enjoying a friendship with the Medici in Florence (who taught them how to become successful bankers). This ushered in a time of stability and peace, when the region's major city-states were run by banking families, and money was freed up for the Renaissance generation to make art, not war.

This square also held the Palace of Justice (the 16th-century courthouse with the clock tower), the market (not food, but crafts: leather, gold, and iron goods), the bank, the city's first university, and its prison. All the elements of a great city were right here on the "Square of the Merchants."

ON PIAZZA DELLA SCALA

To reach these sights, cut through the Galleria Vittorio Emanuele II from Piazza del Duomo.

Piazza della Scala

This smart little traffic-free square, between the Galleria and the opera house, is dominated by a statue of Leonardo da Vinci. The statue (from 1870) is a reminder that Leonardo spent his best 20 years in Milan, where he found well-paid, steady work. He was the brainy darling of the Sforza family (who dominated Milan as the Medici family dominated Florence). Under the great Renaissance genius stand four of his greatest "Leonardeschi." (He apprenticed a sizable group of followers.) The reliefs show his various contributions as a painter, architect, and engineer. Leonardo, wearing his hydro-engineer hat, re-engineered Milan's canal system, complete with locks. (Until the 1920s, Milan was one of Italy's major ports, with canals connecting the city to the Po River and Lake Maggiore.)

The statue of Leonardo is looking at a plain but famous Neoclassical building, arguably the world's most prestigious opera house (described next).

▲▲La Scala Opera House and Museum

Milan's famous Teatro alla Scala opened in 1778 with an opera by Antonio Salieri (Mozart's wannabe rival). Today, opera buffs can get a glimpse of the theater and tour the adjacent museum's extensive collection.

Cost and Hours: Museum—€7, daily 9:00-12:30 & 13:30-17:30, Piazza della Scala, tel. 02-8879-7473, www.teatroallascala.org.

Museum: Well-described in English, the collection features Verdi's top hat, Rossini's eyeglasses, Toscanini's baton, Fettuccini's pesto, original scores, diorama stage sets, busts, portraits, and death masks of great composers and musicians. Upstairs are several tidy rooms of a music library, often displaying costumes. The main reason to visit is the opportunity (on most days) to peek into the actual theater. The stage is as big as the seating area on the ground floor. (You can see the towering stage box from Piazza della Scala across the street.) A recent five-year renovation corrected acoustical problems caused by WWII bombing and subsequent reconstruction.

The royal box is just below your vantage point, in the center rear. Don't overlook the massive chandelier made of Bohemian crystal.

Events in the Opera House: The show goes on at the world-famous La Scala Opera House, which also hosts ballet and classical concerts. There are performances in every month except August, and show time usually is at 20:00 (for information, check online or call Scala Infotel Service, daily 9:00-18:00, tel. 02-7200-3744). On the opening night of an opera, a dress code is enforced for men (suit and tie).

Advance Booking: Seats sell out quickly. Online tickets go on sale two months before performances (www.teatroallascala.org). You can also book through an automated phone system: Call 02-860-775 and press 2 for English. Tickets are also sold at an office beneath Piazza del Duomo (daily 12:00-18:00, use stairs down in front of the Duomo and follow *ATM Point* signs). The "evening box office" *(Biglietteria Serale)* at the opera house itself—see below—opens two hours before show time.

Same-Day Tickets: On performance days, 140 sky-high, restricted-view, peanut-gallery tickets are offered at a low price (generally less than €15) at the box office (located down the left side of the theater toward the back on Via Filodrammatici, and marked with *Biglietteria Serale* sign). It's a bit complicated: You have to show up with an official ID (a driver's license or passport) at 13:00 to put your name on a list (one ticket per person), then return at 17:00 for the roll call. You must be present when your name is called to receive a voucher, which you'll then show at the window to purchase your ticket. (Matinees and symphonic concerts follow a different timetable; check the details on website.) Finally, one hour before show time, the box office sells any remaining tickets at a 25 percent discount.

▲Gallerie d'Italia

This museum fills three adjacent buildings on Piazza della Scala with the amazing art collections of a bank that once occupied part

of this space. The bank building's architecture is early 20th-century, Tiffany-like Historicism, with a hint of Art Nouveau; it's connected to two impressive palazzos that boast the nicest Neoclassical interiors I've seen in Milan. They are filled with exqui-site work by 19th- and 20th-century Italian painters.

Cost and Hours: €5, more during special exhibitions, includes audioguide, Tue-Sun 9:30-19:30, Thu until 22:30, closed Mon, last entry 1 hour before closing, across from La Scala Opera

House at Piazza della Scala 6, toll-free tel. 800-167-619, www. gallerieditalia.com.

Visiting the Museum: Enter through the bank building facing Piazza della Scala and take the red-velvet stairs to the basement to pick up an audioguide (also downstairs is a bag check, WCs, and the original bank vault, which now stores racks and racks of paintings not on display).

Back upstairs, head into the main atrium of the bank, and consider the special exhibits displayed there. Then, to tackle the permanent art collection in chronological order, head to the far end of the complex and work your way back (follow signs for *Palazzo Anguissola Antona Traversi* and *Palazzo Brentani*). You'll go through the café back into the Neoclassical palaces, where you'll trace the one-way route through the "Da Canova a Boccioni" exhibit, including marble reliefs by the Neoclassical sculptor Antonio Canova and Romantic paintings by Francesco Hayez. Upstairs, you'll see dramatic and thrilling scenes from the unification of Italy, as well as beautiful landscapes and cityscapes, especially of Milan. (An entire room is devoted to depictions of the now-trendy Naviglio Grande canal area in its workaday prime.)

On your way back to the bank building and the rest of the exhibit, take a moment to poke around the courtyard to find the *officina di restituzioni alle gallerie*—a lab where you can watch art restorers at work. Picking up the rest of the permanent exhibit, you'll see paintings from the late-19th and early-20th centuries: Romantic landscapes; hyperrealistic, time-travel scenes of folk life; and Impressionism. Finally you'll catch up to the contemporary art of the late 20th century, tucked between old bank teller windows.

WEST OF THE DUOMO

These sights are listed roughly in the order you'll reach them, as you travel west from Piazza del Duomo. The first one is just a few short blocks from the cathedral, while the last is just over a mile away.

▲Pinacoteca Ambrosiana

This oldest museum in Milan was inaugurated in 1618 to house Cardinal Federico Borromeo's painting collection. It began as a teaching academy, which explains its many replicas of famous works of art. Highlights include original paintings by Botticelli, Caravaggio, and Titian—and, most important, a huge-scale sketch by Raphael and a rare oil painting by Leonardo da Vinci.

Cost and Hours: €15, Tue-Sun 10:00-18:00, closed Mon, last entry at 17:00, audioguide-€3, near Piazza del Duomo at Piazza Pio XI 2, Metro: Duomo or Cordusio, tel. 02-8069-2248, www. ambrosiana.eu.

Visiting the Museum: Pick up the English-language map

locating the rooms and major works I highlight below, and rent the audioguide (covers both permanent and special exhibits). Then head upstairs to begin your visit.

Raphael's Cartoon (Room 5): Filling an entire wall, this drawing served as an outline for Raphael's famous *School of Athens* fresco at the Vatican Museums. (A cartoon—*cartone* in Italian—is a full-size sketch that's used to transfer a design to another surface.) While the Vatican's much-adored fresco is attributed entirely to Raphael, it was painted mostly by his students. But this *cartone* was wholly sketched by the hand of Raphael. To transfer the fresco design to the wall, his assistants riddled this cartoon with pinpricks along the outlines of the figures, stuck it to the wall of the pope's study, and then applied a colored powder. When they removed the *cartone,* the figures' shapes were marked on the wall, and completing the fresco was a lot like filling in a coloring book. Also in this room, look for Caravaggio's naturalistic *Basket of Fruit.*

Jan Brueghel (Room 7): As Cardinal Borromeo was a friend of Jan Brueghel, this entire room is filled with delightful works by the artist and other Flemish masters. Study the wonderful detail in Brueghel's *Allegory of Fire* and *Allegory of Water.* The Flemish paintings are extremely detailed—many are painted on copper to heighten the effect—and offer an insight into the psyche of the age. If the cardinal were asked why he enjoyed paintings that celebrated the secular life, he'd likely say, "Secular themes are God's book of nature."

Leonardo Hall (Room 24): During his productive Milan years, Leonardo painted *Portrait of a Musician*—as delicate, mysterious, and thought-provoking as the *Mona Lisa.* (This is the only one of his canvases that remains in Milan.) The large fresco filling the far wall—with Christ receiving the crown of thorns—is by Bernardino Luini, one of Leonardo's disciples. But I find the big replica painting of *The Last Supper* most interesting. When the cardinal realized that Leonardo's marvelous frescoed original was fading, he commissioned a careful copy to be created here for posterity. Today, this copy gives a rare chance to appreciate the original colorful richness of the now-faded masterpiece.

Piazza degli Affari and a Towering Middle Finger

This square and monument mark the center of Milan's financial district. The bold fascist buildings in the neighborhood were built in the 1930s under Mussolini. Italy's major stock exchange, the Borsa, faces the square. Stand in the center and appreciate the modern take on ancient aesthetics (you're standing atop the city's ancient Roman theater). Find the stern statues representing various labors and occupations, and celebrating the nobility of workers—typical whistle-while-you-work fascist themes. Then notice the equally bold modern statue in the center. After a 2009 contest to find the most appropriate sculpture to grace the financial district, this was the winner. With Italy's crippling financial problems, a sentiment similar to the one that powered the Occupy Movement in the US rumbles in this society as well. Here we see how "the 99 percent" feel when they stand before symbols of corporate power in Italy. (Notice how the finger is oriented—it's the 1 percent, and not the 99 percent, that's flipping the bird.) The 36-foot-tall, Carrara marble digit was made by Maurizio Cattelan, the most famous—or, at least, most controversial—Italian sculptor of our age. *L.O.V.E.*, as the statue is titled, was temporary at first. But locals liked it, and, by popular demand, it's now permanent.

▲Church of San Maurizio
(San Maurizio al Monastero Maggiore)

This church, part of a ninth-century convent built into a surviving bit of Milan's ancient Roman wall, dates from around 1500.

Despite its simple facade, it's a hit with art lovers for its amazing cycle of Bernardino Luini frescoes. Stepping into this church is like stepping into the Sistine Chapel of Lombardy.

Cost and Hours: Free, Tue-Sat 9:30-17:30, Sun 13:30-17:30, closed Mon, Corso Magenta 15 at the Monastero Maggiore, Metro: Cadorna or Cairoli, tel. 02-8645-0011.

Visiting the Church: Bernardino Luini (1480-1532), a follower of Leonardo, was also inspired by his contemporaries Michelangelo and Raphael. Sit in a pew and take in the art, which has the movement and force of Michelangelo and the grace and calm beauty of Leonardo.

Maurizio, the patron saint of this church, was a third-century Roman soldier who persecuted Christians, then converted, and eventually worked to stop those same persecutions. He's the guy standing on the pedestal in the upper right, wearing a bright yellow cape. The nobleman who paid for the art is to the left of the altar. His daughter, who joined the convent here and was treated as a queen (as nuns with noble connections were), is to the right. And all around are martyrs—identified by their palm fronds.

The adjacent **Hall of Nuns** (Coro delle Monache), a walled-off area behind the altar, is where cloistered sisters could worship apart from the general congregation. Fine Luini frescoes appear above and around the wooden crucifix. The Annunciation scene at the corners of the arch features a cute Baby Jesus zooming down from heaven (see Mary, on the right, ready to catch him). The organ dates from 1554, and the venue, with its fine acoustics, is popular for concerts with period instruments. Explore the pictorial Bible that lines the walls behind the wooden seats of the choir. Luini's landscapes were groundbreaking in the 16th century. Leonardo incorporated landscapes into his paintings, but Luini was among the first to make landscape the main subject of the painting.

Nearby: You'll exit the Hall of Nuns into the lobby of the adjacent **Archaeological Museum,** where you can pay €5 to see part of the ancient city wall and a third-century Roman tower.

▲▲Basilica di Sant'Ambrogio

One of Milan's top religious, artistic, and historic sights, this church was first built on top of an early Christian martyr's cemetery by St. Ambrose around A.D. 380, when Milan had become the capital of the fading (and Christian) western Roman Empire.

Cost and Hours: Free, Mon-Sat 10:00-12:30 & 14:30-18:30, Sun 15:00-18:00, Piazza Sant'Ambrogio 15, Metro: Sant'Ambrogio, tel. 02-8645-0895, www.basilicasantambrogio.it.

Visiting the Church: Ambrose was a local bishop and one of the great fathers of the early Church. Besides his writings, he's remembered for converting and baptizing St. Augustine of Hippo, who himself became another great Church father. The original fourth-century church was later (in the 12th century) rebuilt in the Romanesque style you see today.

As you step "inside" from the street, you emerge into an arcaded **atrium**—standard in many churches back when you couldn't actually enter the church until you were baptized. The unbaptized waited here during Mass. The courtyard is textbook Romanesque, with playful capitals engraved with fanciful animals. Inset into the wall (right side, above the pagan sarcophagi) are stone markers of Christian tombs—a reminder that this church, like St. Peter's at the Vatican, is built upon an ancient Roman cemetery.

From the atrium, marvel at the elegant 12th-century **facade,** or west portal. It's typical Lombard medieval style. The local bishop would bless crowds from its upper loggia. As two different monastic communities shared the church and were divided in their theology, there were also two different bell towers.

Step into the **nave** and grab a pew. The mosaic in the apse features Jesus Pantocrator (creator of all) in the company of Milanese saints. Around you are pillars with Romanesque capitals and surviving fragments of the 12th-century frescoes that once covered the church.

The 12th-century **pulpit** sits atop a Christian sarcophagus dating from the year 400. Study its late Roman and early Christian iconography—on the side facing the altar, Apollo on his chariot morphs into Jesus on a chariot. You can see the moment when Jesus gave the Old Testament (the first five books, anyway) to his apostles.

The precious, ninth-century golden **altar** has four ancient porphyry columns under an elegant Romanesque 12th-century canopy. The entire ensemble was taken to the Vatican during World War II to avoid destruction. That was smart—the apse took a direct hit in 1943. A 13th-century mosaic was destroyed; today we see a reconstruction.

Step into the **crypt,** under the altar, to see the skeletal bodies of three people: Ambrose (in the middle, highest) and two earlier Christian martyrs whose tombs he visited before building the church.

Nearby: For a little bonus after visiting the church, consider this: The **Benedictine monastery** next to the church is now Cattolica University. With its stately colonnaded courtyards designed by Renaissance architect Donato Bramante, it's a nice place to study. It's fun to poke around and imagine being a student here.

▲Leonardo da Vinci National Science and Technology Museum (Museo Nazionale della Scienza e Tecnica "Leonardo da Vinci")

The spirit of Leonardo lives here. Most tourists focus on the hall of Leonardo—the core of the museum—where wooden models illustrate his designs. But the rest of this immense collection of industrial cleverness is fascinating in its own right. There are exhibits on space exploration, mining, and radio and television (with some original Marconi radios); old musical instruments, computers, and telephones; chunks of the first transatlantic cable; and interactive science workshops (most with English descriptions). Out back are several more buildings containing antique locomotives and a 150-foot-long submarine from 1957. Ask for an English museum map from the ticket desk—you'll need it. On weekends, this museum is very popular with families, so come early or be prepared to wait in line.

Cost and Hours: €10, Tue-Sun 9:30-17:00, Sat until 18:30, closed Mon, Via San Vittore 21, Metro: Sant'Ambrogio; tel. 02-485-551, www.museoscienza.org.

▲▲Leonardo da Vinci's *The Last Supper* (*L'Ultima Cena/Cenacolo Vinciano*)

Decorating the former dining hall *(cenacolo)* of the Church of Santa Maria delle Grazie, this remarkable, exactingly crafted fresco by Leonardo da Vinci is one of the ultimate masterpieces of the Renaissance. Reservations are mandatory and must be booked several months in advance if you want to get in (see reservation options below).

Cost and Hours: €8, includes €1.50 reservation fee (9:30 and 15:30 visits require €3.50 extra for provided English tour). Open Tue-Sun 8:15-18:45 (last entry), closed Mon. Show up 20 minutes before your scheduled entry time. When an attendant calls your time, get up and move into the next room.

Reservations: Mandatory timed-entry reservations can be made either online or by phone (through an outfit called Vivaticket). Reservations for each calendar month go on sale about three months ahead; for example, bookings for July open in early April. Spots are snapped up quickly, so plan ahead.

To book **online,** head to www.vivaticket.it, then choose "Cenacolo Vinciano." A calendar will show available time slots for the coming months.

If you book by **phone,** you'll have a greater selection of days and time slots to choose from, since the website doesn't reflect cancellations. Note that you can't reserve same-day tickets (tel. 02-9280-0360, from the US dial 011-39-02-9280-0360, office open Mon-Sat 8:00-18:30, closed Sun; the number is often busy—once you get through, select 2 for an English-speaking operator).

Tour Option: If you can't get a reservation, you can book a more expensive (€60-75) walking or bus tour that includes a guided visit to *The Last Supper.* These should be reserved at least a few days ahead (for details, see "Tours in Milan," earlier).

Last-Minute Tickets: A few scattered spots may be available same-day due to cancellations. It's a low-percentage play, but you can try just showing up and asking at the desk—even if the *sold out* sign is posted (ideally when the office opens at 8:00, more likely on weekdays). You may get lucky—but don't count on it.

Audioguide: Consider the fine €3.50 audioguide. Its spiel fills every second of the time you're in the room—so try to start listening just before you enter (ideally in the waiting room while studying the reproduction of *The Last Supper*).

Getting There: The Church of Santa Maria della Grazie is a five-minute walk from either Metro: Cadorna or Conciliazione. Or take tram #16 from the Duomo (direction: San Siro or Piazzale Segesta), which drops you off in front of the church.

Photography: No photos are allowed.

Background: Milan's leading family, the Sforzas, hired Leonardo to decorate the dining hall of the Dominican monastery that adjoins the church (the Dominican order traditionally placed a Last Supper on one end of their refectories, and a Crucifixion at the other). Leonardo worked on the project from about 1492 until 1498. This gift was essentially a bribe to the monks so that the Sforzas could place their family tomb in the church. Ultimately, the French drove the Sforzas out of Milan, they were never buried here, and the Dominicans got a great fresco for nothing.

Deterioration began within six years of *The Last Supper's* completion because Leonardo painted on the wall in layers, as he would on a canvas, instead of applying pigment to wet plaster in the usual fresco technique. The church was bombed in World War II, but—miraculously, it seems—the wall holding *The Last Supper* remained standing. A 21-year restoration project (completed in 1999) peeled away 500 years of touch-ups, leaving Leonardo's masterpiece faint but vibrant.

Visiting *The Last Supper:* To minimize damage from humidity, only 30 tourists are allowed in, every 15 minutes for exactly 15 minutes. While you wait, read the history of the masterpiece. As your appointed time nears, you'll be herded between several rooms to dehumidify, while doors close behind you and open up slowly in front of you.

And then the last door opens, you take a step, you look right, and...there it is. In a big, vacant whitewashed room, you'll see faded pastels and not a crisp edge. The feet under the table look like negatives. But the composition is dreamy—Leonardo captures the psychological drama as the Lord says, "One of you will betray me," and the apostles huddle in stressed-out groups of three, wondering, "Lord, is it I?" Some are scandalized. Others want more information. Simon (on the far right) gestures as if to ask a question that has no answer. In this agitated atmosphere, only Judas (fourth from left and the only one with his face in shadow)—clutching his 30 pieces of silver and looking pretty guilty—is not shocked.

The circle meant life and harmony to Leonardo. Deep into a study of how life emanates in circles—like ripples on a pool hit by a pebble—Leonardo positioned the 13 characters in a semicircle. Jesus is in the center, from whence the spiritual force of God emanates, or ripples out.

The room depicted in the painting seems like an architectural extension of the church. The disciples form an apse, with Jesus as the altar—in keeping with the Eucharist. Jesus anticipates his sacrifice, his face sad, all-knowing, and accepting. His feet even foreshadow his death by crucifixion. Had the door, which was cut out in 1652, not been added, you'd see how Leonardo placed Jesus' feet atop each other, ready for the nail.

The perspective is mathematically correct, with Jesus' head as the vanishing point where the converging sight lines meet. In fact, restorers found a tiny nail hole in Jesus' left eye, which anchored the strings Leonardo used to establish these lines. The table is cheated out to show the meal. Notice the exquisite lighting. The walls are lined with tapestries (as they would have been), and the one on the right is brighter in order to fit the actual lighting in the refectory (which has windows on the left). With the extremely natural effect of the light and the drama of the faces, Leonardo created a masterpiece.

NORTH OF THE DUOMO
▲Brera Art Gallery (Pinacoteca di Brera)
Milan's top collection of Italian paintings (13th-20th century) is world-class, but it can't top Rome's or Florence's. Established in 1809 to house Napoleon's looted art, it fills the first floor above a prestigious art college. You'll dodge scruffy starving artists here... and wonder if there's a 21st-century Leonardo in your midst.

Cost and Hours: €6, more during special exhibits, free first Sun of month, Tue-Sun 8:30-19:15, closed Mon, last entry 45 minutes before closing, audioguide-€5 (useful as English information is limited), free lockers, no flash photos, Via Brera 28, Metro: Lanza or Montenapoleone, tel. 02-722-631, www.brera.beniculturali.it.

Visiting the Museum: Enter the grand courtyard of a former monastery, where you'll be greeted by the nude *Napoleon with Tinkerbell* (by Antonio Canova). Climb the stairway (following signs to *Pinacoteca*), buy your ticket, and pick up an English map of the museum's masterpieces, some of which I've highlighted below.

You'll follow a clockwise, chronological route through the huge collection.

Rooms IV-VI: Examine the altar paintings by late-Gothic master Gentile da Fabriano, hinting at the realism of the coming Renaissance (check out the lifelike flowers and realistic, bright gold paint—he used real gold powder). In the darkened section at the far-left end of Room VI, don't miss Andrea Mantegna's tour-de-force, *The Dead Christ.* It's a textbook example of feet-first foreshortening.

Room IX: To experience the peak of 16th-century Venetian painting, check out the color-rich canvases by the great masters Tintoretto and Veronese.

Room XVIII: Stop by the glass-enclosed restoration lab to watch various conservation projects in progress.

Rooms XXI-XXIX: Here you can see how Carlo Crivelli, a contemporary of Leonardo, employed Renaissance technique while clinging to the mystique of the Gothic Age (that's why I like him so much). In the next few rooms, don't miss Raphael's *Wedding of the Madonna* (Room XXIV), Piero della Francesca's *Madonna and Child with Saints* (also Room XXIV), and the gritty-yet-intimate realism of Caravaggio's *Supper at Emmaus* (Room XXIX).

Rooms XXXI-XXXV: Here you'll see Dutch and Flemish masters, including a big Rubens (Room XXXI) and a small Rembrandt (Room XXXIII). Room XXXV displays several of Canaletto's picture-postcards of Venetian cityscapes. This is ahead-of-its-time Impressionism—there's not a single line in these works, just strategically placed daubs of paint.

Room XXXVII: You'll greet the modern age with Giuseppe Pellizza da Volpedo's rousing *Human Flow,* a study for his famous *Fourth Estate* (exhibited at the Museo del Novecento). Also in this room, spice things up with Francesco Hayez's hot and heavy *The Kiss (Il Bacio).*

Risorgimento Museum

With a quick 30-minute swing through this quiet one-floor museum, you'll get an idea of the interesting story of Italy's rocky road to unity: from Napoleon (1796) to the victory in Rome (1870). You'll see paintings, uniforms, monuments, a city model, and other artifacts. But limited English makes this best left to people already familiar with this important period of Italian history.

Cost and Hours: €5, Tue-Sun 9:00-13:00 & 14:00-17:30, closed Mon, just around the block from the Brera Art Gallery at Via Borgonuovo 23, Metro: Montenapoleone, tel. 02-8846-4176, www.museodelrisorgimento.mi.it.

Poldi Pezzoli Museum

This classy house of art features Italian paintings of the 15th through 18th century, old weaponry, and lots of interesting decorative arts, such as a roomful of old sundials and compasses. It's all on view in a sumptuous 19th-century residence.

Cost and Hours: €10, Wed-Mon 10:00-18:00, closed Tue, last entry one hour before closing, English audioguide-€1, Via Manzoni 12, Metro: Montenapoleone, tel. 02-794-889, www. museopoldipezzoli.it.

Bagatti Valsecchi Museum

This unique 19th-century collection of Italian Renaissance furnishings was assembled by two aristocratic brothers who spent a wad turning their home into a Renaissance mansion.

Cost and Hours: €9 includes audioguide, €6 on Wed; open Tue-Sun 13:00-17:45, closed Mon; Via Gesù 5, Metro: Montenapoleone, tel. 02-7600-6132, www.museobagattivalsecchi.org.

SFORZA CASTLE AND NEARBY
▲Sforza Castle (Castello Sforzesco)

The castle of Milan tells the story of the city in brick. Today it features a vast courtyard, a sprawling museum (with a few worthwhile highlights and Leonardo da Vinci connections), and—most important—a chance to see Michelangelo's final, unfinished *pietà*.

Cost and Hours: €5, free entry after 16:30 (Fri after 14:00); open Tue-Sun 9:00-17:30, closed Mon, last entry at 17:00; WCs and free/mandatory lockers downstairs from ticket counter, English info fliers throughout and at information office beside the Porta Umberto entrance, Metro: Cairoli or Lanza, tel. 02-8846-3700, www.milanocastello.it.

Background: Built in the late 1300s as a military fortress, Sforza Castle guarded the gate to the city wall and defended Milan from enemies "within and without." It was beefed up by the Sforza duke in 1450 in anticipation of a Venetian attack. Later, the Sforza family made it their residence, building their Renaissance palace into the fortress. It was even home to their in-house genius, Leonardo. (When he applied for a position with the Sforza family, he did so as a military engineer and contributed to the design of the ramparts.) During the time of foreign rule (16th-19th century), it was a barracks for occupying Spanish, French, and Austrian soldiers. Today it houses an array of museums, but I'd concentrate on the Michelangelo *pietà* and the Museum of Ancient Art.

�𝄞 Self-Guided Tour: This tour begins outside the fortress, then focuses on the highlights inside.

The Fortress: The **gate** facing the city center stands above a ditch that was once filled with water. A relief celebrates Umberto I, the second king of Italy. Above that, a statue of St. Ambrose, the patron of Milan (and a local bishop in the fourth century), oversees the action. Notice the diagram facing the gate that shows how the city was encircled first by a crude medieval wall, and then by a state-of-the-art 16th-century wall—of which this castle was a key element. It's apparent from the enormity of these walls that Milan was a strategic prize. Today, the walls are gone, giving the city two circular boulevards.

This immense brick fortress—exhausting at first sight—can only be described as heavy. Its three huge courtyards originally functioned as military parade grounds, but today host concerts and welcome the public. (The holes in the walls were for scaffolding.)

• *As you enter the main courtyard, look to your left to see the restored hospital building that houses the...*

Museo Pietà Rondanini (Michelangelo): This is a rare opportunity to enjoy a Michelangelo statue with relatively few crowds. Michelangelo died while still working on this piece, his fourth *pietà*—a representation of a dead Christ with a sorrowful Virgin Mary. While unfinished and seemingly a mishmash of corrections and reworks, it's a thought-provoking work by a genius at nearly 90 years old, who knows he's fast approaching the end of his life. The symbolism is of life and of death: Jesus returning to his mother, as two bodies seem to become one.

Michelangelo's more famous *pietà* at the Vatican (carved when he was in his 20s) features a beautiful, young, and astonished Mary. Here, Mary is older and wiser. Perhaps Mary is now better able to accept death as part of life...as is Michelangelo. The *pietà* at the Vatican is simple and clear, showing two different people: the mother holding her dead son. Contemplating the *Pietà Rondanini,* you wonder who's supporting whom. It's confused and complex, each figure seeming to both need and support the other.

This unfinished statue shows the genius of Michelangelo midway through a major rework—Christ's head is cut out of Mary's right shoulder, and an earlier arm is still just hanging there. Above

Mary's right ear, you can see the remains of a previous face (eye, brow, and hairline).

And there's a certain power to this rawness. Walk around the back to see the strain in Mary's back (and Michelangelo's rough chisel work) as she struggles to support her son. The sculpture's elongated form hints at the Mannerist style that would follow.

Facing the *pietà* is a bronze, life-size head, based on a death mask made at the artist's passing in 1564. Imagine him working on his *pietà*—still vibrant and seeking.

• *From the* pietà, *go over the little drawbridge in the back wall—directly across from where you entered the complex. Here you'll find the entrance to the...*

Museum of Ancient Art (Museo d'Arte Antica): This sprawling collection fills the old Sforza family palace with interesting medieval armor, furniture, early Lombard art, and much more.

In the first room, among ancient sarcophagi (with early Christian themes), stands a fine 14th-century **equestrian statue**—a memorial to Bernabò Visconti. Of the four virtues, he selected only two (strength and justice) to stand beside his anatomically correct horse, opting out of love and patience.

Farther along, the room of **tapestries** is dominated by a big embroidery of St. Ambrose defeating the heretical Arians. While that was a fourth-century struggle, 12 centuries later, he was summoned back in spirit to deal with Protestants, in the form of Archbishop Borromeo. As a Counter-Reformation leader, with St. Peter's Basilica behind him, Ambrose stands tall and strong in defense of the Roman Church. The room is lined by 16th-century Flemish tapestries, which were easy to pack up quickly as the nobility traveled. These were typical of those used to warm chilly stone palaces.

Next, you'll come to the **Sala Alberata** ("tree-lined room"). The Visconti family grew rich making silk in the Lake Como area. While plastered over for centuries, this room was restored around 1900. Not much sparkle survives, but you can appreciate the intricate canopy woven with branches and rope in complicated knots— the work of Leonardo himself, in 1498. The tiny Leonardo-esque painting of Madonna and Child is by Francesco Napoletano, a pupil of Leonardo. The painting's structure, anatomy, and subtle modeling of the color with no harsh lines *(sfumato)* are all characteristic of Leonardo. In the upper right, notice the castle, as it looked in 1495.

From here, you'll pass through rooms filled with weapons and armor from the 16th and 17th centuries.

• *At this point, you're free to go. But if you have a larger-than-average attention span, follow signs upstairs to the Decorative Arts Museum, then the Painting Gallery (Pinacoteca), and finally the Musical Instruments Museum (all well-described in English). When you're done, consider popping out the back door of the fortress and taking a break in the lush Sempione Park (described next).*

Parco Sempione

This is Milan's equivalent of Central Park. With its circa 1900 English-style gardens, free Liberty-Style aquarium, views of the triumphal arch, and sprawling family-friendly grounds, this park is particularly popular on weekends.

A five-minute walk through the park, on the left, is the erector-set **Branca Tower** (Torre Branca), built for an exposition in the 1930s. For an inexpensive, commanding city view, you can ride an elevator as high as the Mary that crowns the Duomo (best in daylight, erratic hours—call or confirm at TI before heading out Viale Alemagna, Metro: Cadorna, tel. 02-331-4120).

Next to the tower is the excellent **Triennale di Milano,** a design museum with changing exhibits that celebrate one of this city's fortes (www.triennale.org).

At the far end of the park is the monumental **Arco della Pace.** Originally an arch of triumph, it comes with Nike, goddess of victory, commanding a six-horse chariot. It was built facing Paris to welcome Napoleon's rule and to celebrate the ideals of the French Revolution, destined to lift Italy into the modern age. When the locals learned Napoleon was just another megalomaniac, they turned the horses around, their tails facing France.

▲Via Dante

This grand pedestrian boulevard and popular shopping street leads from Sforza Castle toward the town center and the Duomo. Via Dante was carved out of a medieval tangle of streets to celebrate Italian unification (c. 1870) and make Milan a worthy metropolis. Consequently, all the facades lining it are relatively new. Enjoy strolling this beautiful people zone, where you'll hear the whir of bikes and the lilting melodies of accordion players instead of traffic noise. Photo exhibits are frequently displayed up and down the street. In front of Sforza Castle, a commanding statue of Giuseppe Garibaldi, a hero of the unification movement, looks down one of Europe's longest pedestrian zones. From here you can walk to the Duomo and beyond (about 1.5 miles), appreciating Italian design both in shop windows and on smartly clothed Milanese.

AWAY FROM THE CENTER

▲Naviglio Grande
(Canal District)

Milan, although far from any major lake or river, has a sizable port, literally called the "Big Canal." Since 1170, boats have been able to sail from Milan to the Mediterranean via the Ticino River (which flows into the Po River on its way to the Adriatic Sea). Five hundred years ago, Leonardo helped design a modern lock system. During the booming Industrial Age in the 19th century—and especially with the flurry of construction after Italian unification—ships used the canals to bring in the marble and stone needed to make Milan the great city it is today. In fact, one canal (filled in during the 1930s) let barges unload stone right at the building site of the great cathedral. In the 1950s, landlocked Milan was the seventh-biggest port in Italy, as its canals aided in rebuilding the bombed-out city. Today, disused train tracks parallel the canal, old warehouse buildings recall the area's working-class heritage, and former workers' tenements—once squalid and undesirable—are being renovated. The once-rough area is trendy, traffic-free, pricey, and thriving with inviting bars and eateries. Come here for dinner or a late-afternoon drink (for recommendations, see "Eating in Milan," later).

Getting There: Ride the Metro to Porta Genova, exit following signs to Via Casale, and walk the length of Via Casale one block directly to the canal. Most bars and restaurants are to the left, on both sides of the canal.

Leonardo's Horse

The largest equestrian monument in the world is a modern reconstruction of a model created in 1482 by Leonardo da Vinci for the

Sforza family. The clay prototype was destroyed in 1499 by invading French forces, who used it for target practice. In 1982, American Renaissance-art collector Charles Dent decided to build the 15-ton, 24-foot-long statue from Leonardo's design, planning to present it to the Italians in homage to Leonardo's genius. Unfortunately, Dent died before the project could be completed. In 1997, American sculptor Nina Akamu created a new clay model that became the template for the final statue; it was unveiled in 1999.

Getting There: The statue (free to view) is at a horse racetrack on the western outskirts of town—ride Metro purple line 5 to San Siro Ippodromo.

▲Monumental Cemetery (Il Cimitero Monumentale)

Europe's most artistic and dreamy cemetery experience, this grand place was built just after unification to provide a suitable final resting spot for the city's "famous and well-deserving men." Any cemetery can be evocative, but this one—with its super-emotional portrayals of the deceased and their heavenly escorts (in art styles c. 1870-1930)—is in a class by itself. It's a vast garden art-gallery of proud busts and grim reapers, heartbroken angels and weeping widows, too-young soldiers and countless old smiles, frozen on yellowed black-and-white photos.

Cost and Hours: Free, Tue-Sun 8:00-18:00, closed Mon, last entry at 17:30, pick up map at the entrance gate, ride Metro purple line 5 to Monumentale, tel. 02-8846-5600.

Shopping in Milan

HIGH FASHION IN THE QUADRILATERAL

For world-class window-shopping, visit the Quadrilateral, an elegant high-fashion shopping area around Via Montenapoleone, northeast of La Scala. This was the original Beverly Hills of Milan. In the 1920s, the top fashion shops moved in, and today it remains *the* place for designer labels. Most shops close Sunday and for much of August. On Mondays, stores open only after 16:00. In this land where fur is still prized, the people-watching is as entertaining as the window-shopping. Notice also the exclusive penthouse apartments with roof gardens high above the scene. Via Montenapoleone and the pedestrianized Via della Spiga are the best streets.

Whether you're gawking or shopping, here's the best route: From La Scala, walk up Via Manzoni to the Metro stop at Montenapoleone, browse down Via Montenapoleone, and cut left on Via Santo Spirito (lined with grand aristocratic palazzos—peek into the courtyard at #7). Across the street, step into the elegant courtyard at #10 to check out the café sitters and their poodles. Continue to the end of Via Santo Spirito, then turn right to window-shop down traffic-free Via della Spiga. After a few short blocks, turn right on Via Sant'Andrea and then left, back onto Montenapoleone, which leads you through a final gauntlet of temptations to Corso Giacomo Matteotti, near the Piazza San Babila. Then (for less-expensive shopping thrills), walk back to the Duomo down the pedestrian-only Corso Vittorio Emanuele II.

NEAR THE DUOMO

For a (slightly) more reasonably priced shopping excursion, step into **La Rinascente**—one of Europe's classic department stores. (As you face the front of the Duomo, it's around the left side.) Simply riding the escalator up and up gives a fun overview of Italian design and marketing. The seventh floor is a top-end food circus with recommended restaurants, terrace views of the Duomo, and a public WC. The store's name translates roughly as "the place reborn" and fits its history. In an earlier life, this was a fine Art Nouveau-style building—until it burned down in 1918. Rebuilt, it was bombed in World War II and rebuilt once again (Mon-Thu 9:30-21:00, Fri-Sat 9:30-22:00, Sun 10:00-21:00, has a VAT refund office, faces north side of the Duomo on Piazza del Duomo).

Heading away from the Duomo, stroll between the arcades on the Corso Vittorio Emanuele II, surrounded by clothing stores and other tempting material pleasures. At Via Passarella, detour to the right to check out **Excelsior,** a bold high-end concept store. Moving walkways take you from level to colorful level with pulsing music and electronic art installations. If you're looking for the perfect €1,000 shirt, you've come to the right place. Otherwise, hit **Eat's Food Market,** a stylish deli in the basement, and pick up a tasty high-design salad to go (daily 9:00-22:00, Galleria del Corso 4, two long blocks behind the Duomo, tel. 027-630-7301).

Double back to the Corso Vittorio Emanuele II to continue shopping all the way to the San Babila Metro station (and the ritzy Quadrilateral area described earlier).

Nightlife in Milan

For evening action, check out the artsy Brera area in the old center, with several swanky sidewalk cafés to choose from and lots of bars that stay open late. Home to the local art university, this district has a sophisticated, lively people-watching scene. Another great neighborhood for nightlife, especially for a younger scene, is Naviglio Grande (canal district), Milan's formerly bohemian, now gentrified "Little Venice" (described earlier; Metro: Porta Genova).

There are always concerts and live music playing in the city at various clubs and concert halls. Specifics change quickly, so it's best to rely on the entertainment information in periodicals from the TI.

Sleeping in Milan

My recommended hotels are all within a few minutes' walk of a Metro station. With Milan's fine subway system, you can get anywhere in town in a flash.

Hotel prices in Milan rise and fall with the convention schedule. In March, April, September, and October, the city can be completely jammed by conventions, and hotel prices go sky-high; it's best to avoid the city entirely at these times if you can (for the

Sleep Code

Abbreviations   (€1 = about $1.10, country code: 39)
S=Single, **D**=Double/Twin, **T**=Triple, **Q**=Quad, **b**=bathroom
Price Rankings
  $$$ **Higher Priced**—Most rooms €150 or more
   $$ **Moderately Priced**—Most rooms €110-150
    $ **Lower Priced**—Most rooms €110 or less

Unless otherwise noted, credit cards are accepted, breakfast is included, free Wi-Fi and/or a guest computer is generally available, and English is spoken. Many towns in Italy levy a hotel tax of €1.50-5 per person, per night (often collected in cash; usually not included in the rates I've quoted). Prices change; verify current rates online or by email. For the best prices, always book directly with the hotel.

convention schedule, see www.fieramilano.it). I've listed regular prices, not the much-higher convention rates.

Summer is usually wide-open, with soft or discounted prices, though many hotels close in August for vacation. Hotels cater more to business travelers than to tourists, so prices and availability are a little better on Fridays and Saturdays.

There are only a few small, family-style hotels left in the center, and the good ones charge top dollar for their location. To save money, consider searching online for a deal at a basic chain hotel (such as Ibis) near a Metro stop.

NEAR THE DUOMO

The Duomo area is thick with people-watching, reasonably priced eateries, and the major sightseeing attractions, but hotel prices are high.

$$$ Hotel Spadari boasts a modern, Art Deco-inspired lobby designed by the Milanese artist Giò Pomodoro ("Joe Tomato" in English). The 40 rooms have billowing drapes, big paintings, and designer doors. It's next to the recommended Peck Gourmet Deli, and two blocks from the Duomo (standard Db-€230-260, deluxe Db-€290-360, skip the pricier suites, 5 percent Rick Steves discount through 2016 when you book directly with the hotel, air-con, elevator, Via Spadari 11, tel. 02-7200-2371, www.spadarihotel.com, reservation@spadarihotel.com).

$$$ Hotel Gran Duca di York, three blocks from the Duomo, is on a stark street of banks and public buildings. Public areas are comfortable and spacious, and the 33 rooms are modern and bright (Sb-€98-128, Db-€170-200, 5 percent Rick Steves discount through 2016 if you book directly with the hotel, air-con, elevator, near Metro stops: Cordusio or Duomo, Via Moneta 1, tel. 02-874-863, www.ducadiyork.com, info@ducadiyork.com).

BETWEEN LA SCALA AND SFORZA CASTLE

These slightly less central places are close to the Via Dante and Via Brera shopping and restaurant scenes.

$$$ Antica Locanda dei Mercanti offers 15 rooms in an 18th-century palazzo. While each room has its own personality (some have kitchens, others have spacious terraces), all have a fresh-flower vibe that embraces old and new—a nice change for business-like Milan (Db-€205, €30 more for fun terrace rooms, check website for deals, air-con, elevator, Via San Tomaso 6, Metro: Cairoli or Cordusio, tel. 02-805-4080, www.locanda.it, locanda@locanda.it, Alex and Eri).

$$ Hotel Star rents 30 rooms that are spacious and comfortable but somewhat dated and gaudy (Sb-€140, Db-€160, best prices if you book direct—check website for deals, interior rooms are quieter, air-con, elevator, usually closed for 2 weeks in mid-Aug, Via dei Bossi 5, Metro: Cordusio, tel. 02-801-501, www.hotelstar.it, hotelstar@hotelstar.it, cheeky Vittoria).

$$ London Hotel is a faded, old-school budget hotel, with a living room-like lobby and 30 basic rooms with tiny bathrooms. It's overpriced for what you get, but in a fine location (S-€80-90, Sb-€90-100, D-€110-140, Db-€130-160, Tb-€170-200, price depends on size of room, best price if you book direct, skip their €8 breakfast and grab something on Via Dante, air-con, elevator, Via Rovello 3, Metro: Cairoli, tel. 02-7202-0166, www.hotellondonmilano.com, info@hotellondonmilano.com, sisters Tanya and Licia).

NEAR *THE LAST SUPPER*

These two hotels are farther from the action in a sleepy, mostly residential zone, but the prices are lower.

$$ Antica Locanda Leonardo, just down the street from *The Last Supper,* has a romantic, Old World vibe and antique furnishings. Its 16 rooms face either a courtyard (cheaper, some street noise) or a tranquil garden (flexible rates but typically courtyard Db-€130, garden Db-€160, more for garden balcony, air-con, elevator, Corso Magenta 78, tel. 02-48014197, www.anticalocandaleonardo.com, info@anticalocandaleonardo.com). From the Duomo area, you can ride tram #16, or take the Metro to either Cadorna or Conciliazione and walk 5 minutes.

$$ B&B Hotel Milano Sant'Ambrogio, part of a chain of budget hotels, has 75 efficient, cookie-cutter rooms. They come with some tram noise (request a quieter one), but are worth considering if you can get a deal (generally Db-€130, breakfast extra for discounted rates, air-con, elevator, Via degli Olivetani 4, Metro: S. Ambrogio, tel. 02-4810-1089, www.hotelbb.com, mi.santambrogio@hotelbb. com). It's on a side street near the Leonardo da Vinci Science Museum, about a five-minute walk from either *The Last Supper* or Basilica Sant'Ambrogio.

NEAR MILANO CENTRALE TRAIN STATION

The train station neighborhood is more practical than characteristic. Its hotels are utilitarian business-class places with prices that bounce all over depending upon the convention schedule; most of the year, many have rooms in the €100-125 range. You'll find more shady characters than shady trees in the parks, and lots of ethnic restaurants and massage parlors as you head away from the immediate vicinity of the station. But it's convenient to trains, the Metro, and airport shuttles, and if you hit it outside of convention times, the prices are hard to beat.

On Via Napo Torriani: This street, a five-minute walk in front of the station, is lined with midrange hotels (exit the station, head straight across the square, then veer left onto Via Napo Torriani). **$$ Hotel Berna** feels like a classic European hotel, with an old-school lobby, uniformed bellhops, and 116 faded rooms with some nice upgrades (Db-about €125, Via Napo Torriani 18, tel. 02-677-311, www.hotelberna.com). **$$ Hotel Garda** is cheaper and less welcoming, with 55 rooms (Db-about €100, email first to get a promo code for a 10 percent discount when booking directly on their website, Via Napo Torriani 21, tel. 02-6698-2626, www. hotelgardamilan.com).

Hostel: **$ Ostello Bello Grande** has converted what was a business-class hotel into a well-priced hostel with hipster flair. About half the rooms are 4- to 6-bed dorms; the rest are private rooms with simple, colorful furnishings. Worth considering even if you're not a hosteler, it comes with an inviting rooftop terrace and a shared kitchen (bunk-about €35, Db-€100, includes breakfast and *aperitivo* happy-hour snacks, air-con, elevator, Via Lepetit 33, tel. 02-670-5921, www.ostellobello.com). With the tracks to your back, leave the station to the left, cross the taxi stand, and then cross the road. The hostel is around the corner from Ristorante Giglio Rosso.

Eating in Milan

Milan's hundreds of trendy bars, delis, *rosticcerie*, and self-service cafeterias cater to people with plenty of taste and more money than time. You'll find delightful eateries all over town (note that many places close during August). To eat mediocre food on a street with great people-watching, choose an eatery on the pedestrian-only

Via Dante. To eat with students in trendy little trattorias, explore the Brera neighborhood (especially the pedestrianized Via Fiori Chiari). To eat well near the Duomo, consider the recommended places listed later.

Some locals like to precede lunch or dinner with an *aperitivo*—a before-meal drink (while Campari made its debut in Milan, a simple glass of *vino bianco* or prosecco, the Italian champagne, is just as popular). At about 17:00, bars fill their counters with inviting baskets of munchies, served free with these drinks. If you're either likable or discreet, a cheap drink can become a light meal. This *aperitivo* custom is common throughout Italy but especially prized by the Milanesi—who claim they invented it.

Milan's signature dishes (often served together) are *risotto alla milanese* and *ossobuco*. The risotto is flavored with saffron, which gives it its intense yellow color. The subtle flavor of the saffron pairs nicely with the veal shanks of *ossobuco* (meaning "marrow," or, literally "hole in the bone" shank). The prized marrow, extracted with special little forks, is considered the best part of the meal.

NEAR THE DUOMO
Restaurants with Class

Trattoria Milanese is family-run and traditional, on a dark back street. It has an enthusiastic and local clientele—the restaurant didn't even bother to get a phone until 1988. Expect a Milanese ambience and quality cuisine (€9-11 pastas, €16-22 *secondi*, €25 *ossobuco*, Mon-Sat 12:00-15:00 & 19:00-23:30, closed Sun and mid-July-Aug, evening reservations recommended, air-con, Via Santa Marta 11, near Pinacoteca Ambrosiana, tel. 02-8645-1991).

Ristorante da Bruno serves Tuscan cuisine with a passion for fresh fish. This place impresses with its dressy waiters, hearty food, inexpensive desserts, and a fine self-serve antipasto buffet (a plate full of Tuscan specialties for €10). You can eat inside or on the sidewalk under fascist columns (€10-14 pastas, €16-20 *secondi*, Sun-Fri 12:00-15:00 & 19:00-23:00, closed Sat and Aug, air-con, Via M. Gonzaga 6, reservations wise, tel. 02-804-364, www.ristorantedabruno.biz, Graziella).

Ristorante Calafuria Unione is a thriving Milanese-style eatery that attracts a sizable lunch crowd for its pizza and local dishes. It feels old school, like a well-loved diner (€8-10 pizzas and pastas, €14-20 *secondi*, Mon-Sat 12:00-15:00 & 19:00-24:00, closed Sun, air-con, a few blocks south of Piazza del Duomo at Via dell'Unione 8, Metro: Missori, tel. 02-866-103).

Ronchi 78, a Milan institution for a century, is tight and atmospheric. The main dining room is cozy, while downstairs, more seating sprawls through vaulted cellars. Come here for traditional

MILAN

Hotels & Restaurants in Milan

❶ Hotel Spadari &
   Peck Gourmet Deli
❷ Hotel Gran Duca di York
❸ Antica Locanda dei Mercanti
❹ Hotel Star
❺ London Hotel
❻ To Hotels Berna, Garda &
   Ostello Bello Grande
❼ Trattoria Milanese
❽ Ristorante da Bruno
❾ Ristorante Calafuria Unione
❿ Ronchi 78

⓫ Peck Italian Bar
⓬ Elevator to La Rinascente
   Dep't Store Eateries
⓭ La Vecchia Latteria
⓮ Zime Cafeteria

⑮ Princi Bakeries (2)
⑯ Luini Panzerotti & Cioccolati Italiani
⑰ Via Fiori Chiari Eateries
⑱ Antica Osteria Milanese
⑲ Convivium Ristorante and Pizza

⑳ Bar Brera
㉑ Via Dante Eateries
㉒ To Naviglio Grande Eateries
㉓ Bar Camparino

Milanese cuisine—and, if you're eating late like the Italians do, stay for the nightly "guitarroche" live music (€9-15 pastas, €15-22 *secondi*; cheaper at lunch, closed Sun, Via San Maurilio 7, tel. 02-867-295, www.ronchi78.it).

Peck Italian Bar is a hit with the sophisticated office crowd, which mobs the place at lunch for its fast, excellent meals with im-peck-able service. It's owned by the same people who run the recommended high-end Peck Gourmet Deli (listed later), so be prepared to spend—getting to hang out and be part of the scene makes it worth the money. Any time you find yourself among such a quality-conscious group of Milanesi, you know you're getting good food (€14 pastas, €19-21 *secondi,* no cover, Mon-Fri 7:30-22:00, Sat 9:00-22:00, closed Sun, Via Cantù 3, tel. 02-869-3017, www.peck.it).

Dining with a Duomo View

The seventh floor of La Rinascente department store, alongside the Duomo, has an upscale food court. Three of its many eateries share a sunny outdoor terrace with views of the cathedral's rooftop: **Obicà** is a swanky "mozzarella bar" (part of a chain), offering this heavenly cheese in all its various forms—cow's milk, buffalo, and smoked—in salads, on pizzas, or on splittable €23 antipasto sampler plates, accompanied by *salumi*, tapenades, and vegetables (there are non-mozzarella dishes, too). **Ristorante Maio** has pricey full-meal service. And **Il Bar,** living-room cozy with cushy divans and low coffee tables, serves light meals (salads, pasta), coffee, desserts, and cocktails (all three are expensive—figure €12-16 pastas and pizzas, €20-30 *secondi;* all open daily until 24:00; after store hours, use the elevator on Via S. Radegonda to enter).

Cheaper Eats and Takeout near the Duomo

La Vecchia Latteria, with a 50-year history, is a bright hole-in-the-wall that serves a good vegetarian lunch. This busy joint—with tight seating in front and behind the kitchen—serves soup, salads, pastas, and imaginative veggie entrées at affordable prices. Their star offering is *il misto forno* (small-€13, large-€18, large for two-€30), a delicious assortment of soufflés, quiches, and roasted and sautéed veggies (€9 pastas, Mon-Sat 12:00-16:00, closed Sun, just off Via Torino at Via dell'Unione 6, a few blocks southwest of the Duomo, Metro: Missori, tel. 02-874-401).

Zime cafeteria, in a basement a short walk from the Duomo, is popular with office workers at lunch. Though windowless and a bit noisy, it's inexpensive, authentic, tastefully decorated, and air-conditioned. Decide on one of the set-price combos (€9-11, listed on the wall), and then choose from the dishes on offer

(Mon-Fri 9:00-15:00, closed Sat-Sun, free Wi-Fi; enter the gallery at Via Torino 23, then go downstairs; tel. 02-9163-8484, www.restaurantzime.it).

Princi bakery is mobbed with locals vying for focaccia, olive breadsticks, and luscious pastries. Notice the stacked-wood-oven action in the back. For most pastry items (like the brioche), pay the cashier first; for items sold by weight (such as pizza and cake), get it weighed before you pay. Consider a pasta lunch (12:00-15:00 only) for €6 per plate (open Mon-Sat 7:00-20:00, Sun 9:00-19:30; off Via Torino, a block southwest of Piazza del Duomo at Via Speronari 6; tel. 02-874-797, www.princi.it). Another Princi bakery, more like a café, is near Sforza Castle and is listed later.

Peck Gourmet Deli is an aristocratic deli with a pricey gourmet grocery, *rosticceria*, and pastry/gelato shop on the main level; a fancy restaurant upstairs; and an expensive *enoteca* wine cellar in the basement. Even if all you can afford is the aroma, peek in. Check out the classic circa-1930 salami slicers and the gourmet assembly line in the kitchen in the back. The *rosticceria* serves delectable fancy food to go for a superb picnic dinner. It's sold by weight; order by the *etto*—100-gram unit, 250 grams equals about a half-pound (Mon 15:30-19:30, Tue-Sat 9:30-19:30, closed Sun, Via Spadari 9, tel. 02-802-3161).

Luini Panzerotti, a local institution, is a bakery that serves up piping-hot mini calzones *(panzerotti)* stuffed with mozzarella, tomatoes, ham, or whatever you like for €3-5 (Mon 10:00-15:00, Tue-Sat 10:00-20:00, closed Sun and Aug, Via S. Radegonda 16, tel. 02-8646-1917). From the back of the Duomo, head north and look for the lines out front. Order from the menus posted on the wall behind the cash registers. Traditionally, Milanesi munch their hot little meals on nearby Piazza San Fedele. Don't overlook the *dolci* half of the menu. Across the street is another local hit, **Cioccolati Italiani,** for chocoholics in search of a treat.

EATING NEAR VIA BRERA AND VIA DANTE

These restaurants are near the Cairoli and Lanza Metro stations, and are convenient to Sforza Castle and nearby recommended hotels. The Brera neighborhood, surrounding the Church of St. Carmine, is laced with narrow, inviting pedestrian streets. Make an evening of your visit by having an *aperitivo* with snacks at recommended Bar Brera or any other bar—most serve munchies with drinks from 17:00 until 21:00. Afterward, stroll along restaurant row on Via Fiori Chiari and Via Brera, or duck into the semicircular lane of Via Madonnina to survey the sidewalk cafés as you pass fortune tellers, artists, and knockoff handbag vendors.

Antica Osteria Milanese is a hardworking family place with a smart local following and spacious, stylish seating. They serve good-quality, typical Milanese favorites (€9 pastas, €13-17 *secondi*, Mon-Sat 12:15-14:30 & 19:30-22:15, closed Sun, Via Camperio 12, tel. 02-861-367, www.anticaosteriamilanese.it, Alessandro).

Convivium Ristorante and Pizza is popular for its extensive wine list, clever dishes (especially beef and fish), and conviviality. It's trendy but classy (€9-11 pizza, €9-15 pastas, €19-24 *secondi*, daily 12:00-14:30 & 19:00-24:00, facing Santa Maria del Carmine church at Via Ponte Vetero 21, tel. 02-8646-3708, www.conviviumristorante.it, Claudio and Nicola).

Princi bakery's branch on Via Ponte Vetero works the same as the one on Via Speronari (listed earlier), only it's more like a restaurant, with seating both inside and on the street. While the bakery and café are open all day, their pasta counter (with €6 plates) serves only from 12:00 to 15:00 (Mon-Sat 7:00-20:00, Sun 9:00-20:00, Via Ponte Vetero 10, tel. 02-7201-6067, www.princi.it).

Bar Brera serves €5 sandwiches, €7 pastas, and €8-10 salads to throngs of art students, and has a lively *aperitivo* happy hour (€8 drinks and a buffet of hearty snacks starts at 18:00; open daily 7:00-late, Via Brera 23, tel. 02-877-091).

Fancy Via Dante Bars and Cafés: Thriving and central, Via Dante is lined with hardworking eateries where you can join locals for a lively lunch. Or just swing by for a morning *caffè*, watching the parade of Milanesi heading to work.

IN NAVIGLIO GRANDE (CANAL DISTRICT)

Consider ending your day at the former port of Milan. The Naviglio Grande district bustles with memorable and affordable bars and restaurants and a great people scene. In addition to endless *aperitivo* spreads and traditional trattorias, there are some more creative choices, too: Greek fare, artisanal microbrews, and "Brazilian sushi."

Getting There: Ride the Metro to Porta Genova and walk down Via Casale, which dead-ends a block away at the canal. Walk halfway across the metal bridge and survey the scene. The street you just walked has plenty of cheap options. Most of the action—and all of my other recommendations—are to the left, on or near the canal. Do a reconnaissance stroll before settling in somewhere: Walk down the left bank of the canal to the bridge with cars, then go back on the other side.

Here are a few good options to consider, listed in the order you'll pass them.

Ristorante Brellin is the top romantic splurge, with a dressy crowd and fine food. The menu is international while clinging to a bit of tradition (€14-16 pastas, €22-28 *secondi*, daily 12:30-15:30 & 19:00-24:00; behind the old laundry tubs where a small lane, Vicolo dei Lavandai, branches off from the canal; tel. 02-5810-1351, www.brellin.it).

Pizzeria Tradizionale, at the far end of the walk after you cross the bridge, is a local favorite for pizza (€6-11 pies, Thu-Tue 12:00-14:30 & 19:00-24:00, Wed 19:00-24:00, at the far end of canal walk, Ripa di Porta Ticinese 7, tel. 02-839-5133).

Cucina Fusetti is a charming little place a few doors off the canal serving pan-Mediterranean cuisine, including *bacalao*—salt cod (€12-14 pastas, €18-20 *secondi*, Mon-Sat 19:00-23:00, closed Sun; near the curved bridge with the zigzag design, go away from canal on Via Argelati to Via M. Fusetti 1; mobile 340-861-2676).

Pizzeria Spaghetteria La Magolfa, down a side street, feels like a neighborhood hangout, offering good, cheap €5-9 salads, pastas, and pizzas. You can sit inside, on a veranda, or at a table on the street. For less than €20, two people could split a hearty pizza and a good bottle of wine and get full...and a bit drunk (Mon-Sat 11:00-16:00 & 18:00-24:00, Sun 18:00-24:00, go a long block past Cucina Fusetti to end of street, Via Magolfa 15, tel. 02-832-1696, www.lamagolfa.it).

Milan Connections

BY TRAIN

From Milano Centrale by Train to: Venice (2/hour, most direct on high-speed ES trains, 2.5 hours), **Florence** (hourly, 2 hours), **Genoa** (hourly, 2 hours), **Rome** (2-3/hour, 3-3.5 hours), **Brindisi** (4 direct/day, 2 night trains, 9-15 hours), **Cinque Terre/La Spezia** (hourly, 3 hours direct or with change in Genoa; trains from La Spezia to the villages go nearly hourly), **Cinque Terre/Monterosso al Mare** (8/day direct, otherwise hourly with change in Genoa, 4 hours), **Varenna** on Lake Como (1 hour; small line direct to Lecco/Sondrio/Tirano leaves at :20 past most hours—confirm these times), **Stresa** on Lake Maggiore (about hourly; 50-minute fast train may require reservations, while 1.5-hour train doesn't), **Como** (2/hour, 30-60 minutes, boats go from Como to Varenna until about 19:00), **Naples** (direct trains hourly, 5 hours, more with change in Rome, overnight possible); see www.trenitalia.com for details.

From Milano Porta Garibaldi by High-Speed Train: The Italo rail company offers additional high-speed connections (some direct) to **Florence** (10/day, 2 hours), **Rome** (16/day, 3-3.5 hours), and **Naples** (12/day, 4.5-5 hours). While Italo is often cheaper (particularly if you book long in advance), it doesn't accept rail passes, and you'll have to change stations in Milan if you're connecting to or from anywhere else.

International Destinations: Basel, with connections to

Frankfurt (3/day, 4 hours), **Geneva** (4/day, 4 hours), **Lugano** (almost hourly, 1 hour), **Munich** (night train weekdays only, 9 hours), **Nice** (6/day, change in Ventimiglia, 5 hours), **Paris** (3/day from Milano Porta Garibaldi, 7 hours; daily night train from Milano Centrale, 11 hours), **Vienna** (night train on weekdays only, 11 hours), **Zürich** (4/day, 3 hour).

BY PLANE

To get flight information for Malpensa or Linate airports or the phone number of your airline, call 02-74851 or 02-232-323 and wait for English options, or check www.sea-aeroportimilano.it.

Note: While the train works best for Malpensa, if you want to take a shuttle bus to any of Milan's airports, just go to Milano Centrale station and walk out the door marked *Piazza Luigi di Savoia*. There, you'll find little sales kiosks aggressively selling tickets for all of your options.

Malpensa Airport

Most international flights land at Terminal 1 of the manageable Malpensa Airport (airport code: MXP), 28 miles northwest of Milan. Low-cost EU flights use Terminal 2 (buses connect the two). Both have ATMs and exchange offices. Terminal 1 has a pharmacy, eateries, and a hotel reservation service disguised as a TI. When you leave the baggage-carousel area, go right to reach services and exit (tel. 02-5858-0080).

Trains from Malpensa to Milan: The Malpensa Express train is usually the most sensible way to travel (not covered by rail passes, tel. 800-500-005, www.malpensaexpress.it). Trains leave from an underground station at Terminal 1; buy your ticket from a kiosk in the arrivals hall, or from Trenord ticket machines in the baggage claim hall (credit cards accepted). A big electronic board shows the next departure times. There are two lines: Malpensa-Milano Cadorna and Malpensa-Milano Centrale. For either, the ride costs €12 one-way. Validate your ticket in the little machines, and double-check to make sure your train is going to the destination you want.

If you are headed downtown or to most other points in the city, take the **Cadorna** line, which is quicker, runs more often and later, and drops you at a convenient downtown Metro station (2/hour, 35 minutes; usually departs airport at :28 and :58 past the hour, generally departs Cadorna at :27 and :57 past the hour, last train from airport leaves 1:03 in the morning, first train from Cadorna leaves 4:27).

If you are heading to the area around Milano Centrale train station, or connecting by train to other destinations, take the **Centrale** line (2/hour, 50 minutes, usually departs airport at :05 and :35 past the hour and Milano Centrale at :25 and :55 past the hour, last train from airport leaves 22:43, first train from Milano Centrale leaves 5:25).

If you're **leaving Milan** to go *to* the airport, purchase your ticket before you board, either from the green Trenord ticket machines or, at Cadorna Station, from the staffed ticket windows. At Milano Centrale, trains leave from tracks 2 and 3; ticket machines are at the end of track 3, which is hidden behind track 4, and poorly signed. Cadorna is a little easier to deal with; trains usually depart from track 1.

By Shuttle Bus: Two bus companies run between Malpensa Airport and Milano Centrale train station, offering virtually identical, competing services. They each charge about €10 for the one-hour trip (buy ticket from driver) and depart from the same places: in front of Terminal 2 (outside exit 4) and from Piazza Luigi di Savoia (on the east side of Milan's central train station—with your back to the tracks, exit to the left). They also pick up and drop off at Terminal 1, which, if your flight docks there, makes the bus an option to taking the train. Buses leave about every 20 minutes, every day, from very early until just after midnight (Malpensa Shuttle tel. 02-5858-3185, www.malpensashuttle.it; Autostradale tel. 02-3391-0794, www.autostradale.it).

By Taxi: Taxis into Milan cost a fixed rate of €90; avoid hustlers in airport halls (catch taxis outside exit 6). Considering how far the city is from the airport and how good the train and bus services are, Milan is the last place I'd take an airport taxi.

Linate Airport

Most European flights land at Linate (airport code: LIN), five miles east of Milan. The airport has a bank with an ATM (just past customs) and a hotel-finding service disguised as a TI (daily 7:30-23:30, tel. 02-7020-0443). Eventually the Metro's new line 4 will link Linate with the city. For now, you can get to downtown Milan by bus or taxi.

By Bus: Public bus #73 connects Linate in about 20 minutes to the San Babila Metro station (ride one stop to the Duomo on red line 1 or walk 10 minutes; covered by €1.50 public transit ticket, which is valid for connecting to Metro, departs every 10 minutes, less frequently evenings and Sun). Private companies also run more expensive shuttles to Milano Centrale train station (handy only if you're catching a train; €5, 2/hour, 25 minutes, www.airportbusexpress.it).

By Taxi: Taxis from Linate to the Duomo cost about €25.

Bergamo (Orio al Serio) Airport

Some budget airlines, such as Ryanair and Wizz Air, use Bergamo Airport—about 30 miles from Milan—as their Milan hub (airport code: BGY, tel. 035-326-323, www.sacbo.it). At least three bus companies ply the route between the east side of Milano Centrale train station (Piazza Luigi di Savoia) and Orio al Serio (€5, about 5/hour, 1 hour): Autostradale (www.airportbusexpress.it), Terravision (www.terravision.eu), and the Orio Shuttle (www.orioshuttle.com).

THE LAKES

Commune with nature where Italy is joined to the Alps, in the lovely Italian lakes district. In this land of lakes, the million-euro question is: Which one? For the best mix of accessibility, scenery, and offbeatness, the village of Varenna on Lake Como is my top choice, while Lake Maggiore is a suitable backup. In either place, you'll get a complete dose of Italian-lakes wonder and aristocratic-old-days romance.

You could spend a busy day side-tripping from Milan (about one hour away by train) to either lake, do some island- and villa-hopping, and be home in time for dinner. But the lakes are an ideal place to slow down and take a break from your busy vacation. Settle in here, and bustling Milan doesn't even exist. Now it's your turn to be *chiuso per restauro* (closed for restoration). If relaxation's not on your agenda, the lakes shouldn't be either.

Lake Como

Lake Como (Lago di Como)—lined with elegant 19th-century villas, crowned by snowcapped mountains, and busy with ferries, hydrofoils, and slow, passenger-only boats—is a good place to take a break from the intensity and turnstile culture of central Italy. It seems like half the travelers you'll meet have tossed their itineraries into the lake and are actually relaxing.

Lake Como is Milan's quick getaway, and the sleepy mid-lake village of Varenna is the handiest base of operations. With good connections to other mid-lake towns (and Milan), Varenna is my favorite place to stay on the lake. While Varenna has a village vibe, beautiful Bellagio has earned its ritzy allure and feels a bit more like a real city, making it a good alternative.

The hazy, lazy lake's only serious industry is tourism. Every day, hundreds of lakeside residents commute to work in Lugano, just across the border in Switzerland. The lake's isolation and flat economy have left it pretty much the way the 19th-century Romantic poets described it: heaven on earth.

PLANNING YOUR TIME

Even though there are no essential activities, plan for at least two nights so you'll have an uninterrupted day to see how slow you can get your pulse. Spend some time exploring your home-base town, take my self-guided ferry tour to take in the scenery (with visits to the lake's two main villas), and hop off the boat to poke around the town you're not staying in. With additional time, visit more lakeside villas or go for a hike.

Lake Como is also workable as a day trip from Milan. Take a morning train to Varenna, ride the boat to Lenno (and tour Villa

Balbianello), then take a boat to Villa Carlotta to tour the gardens. From there, head either to Bellagio or back to Varenna to linger and explore (or, with more time and energy, see a little of both) before taking the train back to Milan from Varenna. Start early to pack everything in; otherwise, you'll likely have to be more selective (with time to see just one of the villas).

GETTING TO LAKE COMO

By Train via Varenna: From any destination covered in this book, you'll reach Lake Como via Milan. The quickest, easiest, and cheapest way to get from Milan to any mid-lake town is to take the train to Varenna. From Varenna you can hop on a boat to Bellagio.

At Milan's central train station (Milano Centrale), catch a train heading for Sondrio or Tirano—sometimes the departure board also says "Lecco/Tirano." (Tirano is often confused with Torino...wrong city.) All Sondrio-bound trains stop in Varenna, as noted in the fine print on the *partenze* (departures) schedule posted at Milan's train station. Trains leave Milan nearly hourly at :20 past the hour, but there are a few gaps when a train doesn't leave for two hours (confirm times at station or online at www.trenitalia.com). Get a second-class ticket, since most of these trains don't have first-class cars (rail passes accepted). If you plan to head back to Milan on the train, you might as well also buy a return ticket. Stamp your ticket in the yellow box or risk a €50 fine. If you run into a problem or need to validate your rail pass at Milan's train station, find the helpful Trenitalia office on the ground floor.

Leaving Milan, sit on the left for maximum lake-view beauty. Get off at Varenna-Esino-Perledo. (Even though train schedules list just Varenna or Varenna-Esino, Varenna-Esino-Perledo is what you'll see at the platform.) The long trains that serve Varenna's tiny station stop only briefly—be ready to hop out. The single platform is very narrow, and your car may actually stop before or after the platform. Look out the window. If even part of the train is at the station, you'll need to get out and walk. Tips: Board midtrain to land next to a platform. Leave from the door through which you entered, since you know it's working. If necessary, pull hard on the red handle to open the door.

By Boat via Como: For a less convenient, much slower, but more scenic trip, you can get to Varenna or Bellagio from Milan via the town of Como. Trains take you from Milan to Como (2/hour, 30-60 minutes). From the station in Como, it's a 10-minute walk to the dock, where you catch either the speedy hydrofoil or the leisurely *battello* (slow boat—great for enjoying the scenery) for the ride up the lake to Bellagio or Varenna. Boats leave Como about hourly (slow ferry boat: €11.60, 2.5 hours, last departure about 15:20; hydrofoil: €16.20, 1 hour, last departure about 19:20, fewer on Sun).

Boat Schedule Literacy

Types of Boats

Traghetto or *autotraghetto*	Car and passenger ferry
Aliscafo or *servizio rapido*	Hydrofoil (more expensive, faster, enclosed, and less scenic)
Battello ship	Slow passenger-only boat going all the way to Como
Battello navetta	Shuttle serving mid-lake only

Schedule Terms

Feriali	Monday-Saturday
Festivi	Sundays and holidays
Partenze da...	Departing from...

By Plane via Milan's Airports: Take the Malpensa Express train from Malpensa Airport, the Airport Bus Express from Linate Airport, or any of the buses from Bergamo's Orio al Serio Airport to Milano Centrale train station, and then transfer to a Varenna-bound train.

By Taxi: Taxis between Varenna and Milan or its airports won't save money over the train, even for groups, but can be worth it for the convenience. **Marco Barili** (and his wife Nelly) don't add surcharges for baggage or early/late departures (€140 to central Milan or Linate Airport, €160 to Malpensa Airport for up to 4 people—or €220 for 5-8 passengers in a minibus, €130 to Orio al Serio Airport—or €180 for 5-8 people, tel. 0341-815-061, taxi. varenna@tiscali.it).

GETTING AROUND LAKE COMO

By Boat: Boats go about every 30 minutes between Varenna and Bellagio (€4.60/hop, 15-20 minutes, daily approximately 7:00-22:30). If you're staying in one of these towns, you'll probably limit your cruising to this scenic mid-lake area. Express boats cost

a little more and save only a couple of minutes per leg. Because boats are frequent and the schedule is hard to read, I just show up, buy a ticket for the next boat, and wait. Always ask which slip *(pontile)* your boat will leave from—it's not posted, and Bellagio has several docks (boat info: toll-free tel. 800-551-801 or tel. 031-579-211, www.navigazionelaghi.it). On sunny days, there can be long lines at ticket booths; don't dillydally, and consider buying your tickets in advance at a quieter time. The one-day €15 mid-lake pass makes sense only if you take four or more rides—unlikely (pass does not cover the fast hydrofoils).

If you're making more complex plans, pick up a free **boat schedule** and ask for help to decipher it. It's a good idea to ask your hotelier to help review your possible connections before you set out so you can pace your day smartly. You'll find the schedule at travel agencies, hotels, and boat docks. Confusingly, the schedule requires you to scan four different timetables to know all the departures; for key terms, see the sidebar.

By Car: With scarce parking, traffic jams, and expensive car ferries, this is no place to drive. While it's possible to drive around the lake, the road is narrow, congested, and lined with privacy-seeking walls, hedges, and tall fences. Parking in Bellagio is more difficult than in Varenna. If you do have a car, park it in Varenna, and use the boat to get around.

While you can rent cars in Bellagio, for most travelers, it's best to take the train to Milan and pick up a car there, either at the central train station or at one of Milan's three airports.

Varenna

This well-manicured village of 800 people offers the best of all lake worlds. Easily accessible by train, on the less-driven side of the lake, Varenna has a romantic promenade, a tiny harbor, steep and narrow stepped lanes, and some scenic sights (a ruined castle and two villas). It's just the right place to savor a lakeside cappuccino or *aperitivo*. There's wonderfully little to do here, and it's very quiet at night...unless you're here during one of the hundred or so annual American wedding parties. The *passerella* (lakeside promenade, well-lit and inviting after dark) is adorned with caryatid lovers pressing silently against each other in the shadows. Varenna is a popular destination with my readers and European vacationers—book well in advance for visits in summer (May-Oct). From November to mid-March, Varenna practically shuts down; hotels close for the winter, and restaurants and shops reduce their hours.

Central Lake Como

To Tirano &
St. Moritz
(Switzerland)

Lake Como

12 miles to
Lugano (Switz.)
(scenic bus)

Monte
Grona

Porlezza

Lake
Lugano

S-340

S-340

Bellano

VARENNA-ESINO-
PERLEDO
STATION

CASTELLO DI VEZIO

Varenna

Menaggio

YOUTH
HOSTEL

SOURCE OF RIVER

2 Kilometers

2 Miles

Cadenabbia
Villa Carlotta

Tremezzo

Lenno

Campo

Ospedaletto

Villa
Balbianello

Isola
Comacina

Punta
Sparti-
vento

Pescallo

Bellagio

San
Giovanni

S-583

Lake Como

Fiumelatte
(tiny river)

To Como
S-340

Lake
Como

Area of
Detail

Menaggio

Varenna

Bellagio

Lake
Lecco

Como

Lecco

Lake Lecco

.... Mid-lake Boats
ﬞﬞﬞﬞﬞ Self-guided Ferry Tour
.... Other Boats
–·–·– Rail
– – – Trail

Mandello

To Como
& Milan

To Lecco

To Lecco
& Milan

LAKES

Orientation to Varenna

TOURIST INFORMATION

The TI is on the **main square** (May-Sept Tue-Sat 10:00-13:00 &
14:00-17:30, Sun 10:00-13:00, closed Mon, weekends only Oct-
April, just past the bank at Via IV Novembre 7, tel. 0341-830-367,
varennaturismo.com). The Tivano travel agency, located in the
train station, also operates as a TI (described later, under "Helpful
Hints"). At either TI (or your hotel), pick up the latest edition of
the *Varenna Tourist Info* booklet.

ARRIVAL IN VARENNA

Varenna is small, and pretty much everything is within a 15-min-
ute walk.

By Train: From Varenna's train station, you can **walk** along
the marked pedestrian lane down to the main road. If you're heading for the ferry to Bellagio, go straight; otherwise, turn left along
the main road and keep rolling into town (a 10- to 15-minute walk
from the station; watch for traffic where the sidewalk ends). If you

have a bag with wheels, avoid using the lakeside promenade, which ends in stairs and cobbles.

A **taxi** from the station costs about €9-10. Reliable Marco Barili (or his wife Nelly) can meet you at the train station if you know your exact arrival time in Varenna. Look for a flashing sign with your name on it (tel. 0341-815-061, taxi.varenna@tiscali.it).

By Boat: The boat dock is close to the train station and a 10-minute stroll north of the main square and old town.

By Car: Avoid on-street parking in Varenna; the few spots are mostly reserved for residents. The easiest (though most expensive) option for parking is the spiffy multilevel lot at the south end of town, across from the entrance to Villa Monastero (€2/hour from 6:00 to 22:00, otherwise €1/hour, €20/24 hours).

At the train station, parking is free overnight and Monday-Friday during the day, but you'll have to pay from 9:00 to 20:00 on Saturdays, Sundays, and holidays during high season and every day June through August (€1.20/hour, feed coins into meter in center

❶	Hotel du Lac
❷	Albergo Milano & Ristorante la Vista
❸	Villa Cipressi & Ristorante la Contrada
❹	Hotel Royal Victoria
❺	To Hotel Eremo Gaudio
❻	Albergo/Ristorante del Sole
❼	Albergo Beretta
❽	Hotel Montecodeno
❾	Ristorante il Cavatappi
❿	Osteria Quatro Pass
⓫	Varenna Monamour
⓬	Nilus Bar & Bar Il Molo
⓭	To Ristorante il Caminetto & Cooking Course
⓮	Pub l'Orso
⓯	Vecchia Varenna
⓰	Hotel/Ristorante Olivedo
⓱	Da Luigi Pizza da Re
⓲	Gelateria Riva
⓳	Grocery Stores (2)
⓴	Ornithology & Natural Science Museum
㉑	Laundry
㉒	Barilott Bar (Train Tickets)
㉓	Villa Monastero Entrance

of lot and put ticket on dashboard; €10 day pass available from I Viaggi del Tivano travel agency at the station).

HELPFUL HINTS

Travel Agency: Varenna's travel agency, **I Viaggi del Tivano,** is conveniently located in the train station. In addition to acting as a TI (it's a good place to pick up a town map and boat schedules, browse brochures, and get your questions answered), they book planes, trains, and automobiles (Mon-Fri 9:00-13:00 & 14:30-18:30, Sat-Sun 9:00-16:00, Oct-April closes Sat at 13:00 and all day Sun; no service charge for regional train tickets, €5 booking fee for long-distance train tickets, tel. 0341-814-009, www.tivanotours.com, info@tivanotours.com, helpful Cristina and Eleonora). They also offer half-day and daylong bus and boat tours of the region, including Switzerland (April-Sept only, book tours by noon the day before).

Train Tickets: The train station doesn't have ticket windows, but you can buy tickets at the **I Viaggi del Tivano** travel agency there (see above). Don't cut it too close, in case there's a line. You can also buy tickets at the **Barilott** bar/tobacco shop downtown, which is also a lively place to buy a *panino* and/or a glass of wine and use the Wi-Fi—free for paying customers (Mon-Sat 7:00-20:00, closed Sun, Via IV Novembre 6, tel. 0341-815-045, Claudia and Fabrizio).

Money: One bank is near Varenna's main square; another is located inland from the boat dock. Both have ATMs (see town map).

Post Office: It's at the bottom corner of the main square (Tue and Thu-Fri 8:30-13:45, Sat 8:20-12:45).

Laundry: Lavanderia Pensa Barbara can wash and dry your laundry within 24 hours (priced by weight, figure around €15-18/load, no self-service, closed Sat afternoon and all day Sun, Via Venini 31, tel. 0341-830-478, mobile 340-466-2977). There's also a self-service machine tucked in the back of the little **"Il Bottaio"** shopping mall facing the harbor (daily 8:00-24:00).

Varenna Walk

Since you came here to relax, this short self-guided walk gives you just the town basics.

• *Begin by standing in the little piazza next to the...*

Bridge Just Below Train Station: This main bridge spans the tiny Esino River, which divides two communities: Perledo (which sprawls up the hill—notice the church spire high above) and the old fishing town of Varenna (huddled around its harbor). The train station, called Varenna-Esino-Perledo, gives due respect to both, as well as the village of Esino, eight miles higher in the hills.

Go down the tree-lined promenade on the right (north) side of the river. You'll run into the entrance to the town's public beach—the *lido* (€2 entry)—and then cross the cute pedestrian bridge to the small square, which hosts a market on Wednesdays.

The yellow inn facing the ferry dock, Hotel Olivedo, has greeted ferry travelers since the 19th century and is named for the olive groves you can see growing halfway up the hill. Natives claim this is the farthest north that olives grow in Europe.

• *Across from Hotel Olivedo is Varenna's...*

Ferry Landing: Since the coming of the train in 1892, this has been the main link to Milan and the world for the "mid-lake" communities of Bellagio, Menaggio (described later), and Varenna. From this viewpoint, you can almost see how Lake Como is shaped like a man. The head is the north end (to the right, up by the Swiss Alps). Varenna is the left hip (to the east). Menaggio, across the lake, is the right hip (to the west). And Bellagio (hiding behind the smaller wooded hill to your left) is the crotch—or, more poetically,

Punta Spartivento ("Point that Divides the Wind"). In a more colorful description, a traditional poem says, "Lake Como is a man, with Colico the head, Lecco and Como the feet, and Bellagio the testicles." (In the regional dialect, this rhymes—ask a native to say it for you.)

The farthest ridges high above the right hip mark the border of Switzerland. This region's longtime poverty shaped the local character (much like the Great Depression shaped the outlook of a generation of Americans). Many still remember that the Varenna side of the lake was the poorest, because those on the Menaggio side controlled the lucrative cigarette-smuggling business over the Swiss border. Today, the entire region is thriving—thanks to tourism.

LAKES

• *Walk past the ferry dock and the small playground to Varenna's elevated shoreline walk, called the...*

Passerella: A generation ago, Varenna built this elegant lakeside promenade, which connects the ferry dock with the old town

center. Strolling this lane, you'll come to the tiny, two-dinghy, concrete breakwater of a villa. Lake Como is lined with swanky 19th-century villas; their front doors face the lake to welcome visitors arriving by boat. At this point, the modern *passerella* cuts between this villa's water gate and its private harbor. Just around the bend, enjoy a good Varenna town view. These buildings are stringently protected by preservation laws; you can't even change the color of your villa's paint.

Just over the hump (which allows boats into a covered moorage), look back and up at another typical old villa—with a private *passerella*, a lovely veil of wisteria, and a prime lakeview terrace. Many of these villas are owned by the region's "impoverished nobility." Bred and raised not to work, eventually they were unable to pay for the upkeep of their sprawling houses. Some of these villas have now been bought by the region's nouveau riche.

• *At the community harbor, walk to the end of the pier for a town overview, then continue under the old-time arcades toward the multihued homes facing the harbor.*

Varenna Harborfront: There are no streets in the old town—just the characteristic stepped lanes called *contrade.* Varenna was originally a fishing community. Even today, old-timers enjoy Lake Como's counterpart to Norwegian lutefisk: *missoltino,* air-dried and salted lake "sardines."

Imagine the harbor 200 years ago—busy with coopers fitting chestnut and oak staves into barrels, stoneworkers carving the black marble that was quarried just above town, and fishermen dragging boats onto the sloping beach. The little stone harbor dates from about 1600. Today, the fishing boats are just for recreation, and residents gather here with their kids to relax by the lake.

At the south end of the harbor (in front of the recommended Bar Il Molo), belly up to the banister of the terrace for a colorful town view. Another traditional ditty goes, "If you love Lake Como, you know Bellagio is the pearl...but Varenna is the diamond."

• *Continue straight, leaving the harbor. A lane curves around Hotel du Lac (its fine lakeside terrace welcomes even nonguests for a drink), finishing with an unexpected hill. Finally you'll reach the tiny pebbly town beach below. From here, climb the stairs and go through the yellow arch to the square called...*

Piazza San Giorgio: Several churches face Varenna's town square. The main church (Chiesa di San Giorgio) dates from the 13th century. Romantic Varenna is an understandably popular spot for weddings—rice often litters the church's front yard. Stepping inside, you'll find a few humble but centuries-old bits of carving and frescoes. The black floor and chapels are made from the local marble.

Just past the church and the municipal building is the TI and the Ornithology and Natural Science Museum, with a small collection of stuffed birds and other wildlife (small entry fee, same hours as TI).

The Hotel Royal Victoria, also on the main square, recalls the 1839 visit of Queen Victoria, who registered herself as the Countess of Clare in an attempt to remain anonymous.

The trees in the square are planted to make a V for Varenna. The street plan survives from Roman times, when gutters flowed down to the lake. The little church on the lake side of the square is the baptistery. Dating from the ninth century, it's one of the oldest churches on the lake, but is rarely open for visits.

Your walk is over. Facing the church, you can head right to visit the gardens or to take a demanding hike up to the castle (both described next, under "Sights in Varenna"). You can go left to get to the train station or ferry dock—or for a less-demanding but still steep hike to the castle. Head back downhill to enjoy the beach (take either of the lanes flanking the Hotel Royal Victoria down to the water).

Sights in Varenna

▲Hike to Vezio Castle (Castello di Vezio)

A steep and stony trail leads to Varenna's ruined hilltop castle, located in the peaceful, traffic-free, one-chapel hamlet of Vezio. Take the small road, Via per Vezio (about 100 feet south of—and to the right of—Hotel Montecodeno), and figure on a 20-minute walk one-way. Arriving in Vezio, follow *castello* signs. You'll reach a bar (with drinks, light food, and WCs) that serves as the castle's ticket desk. Once inside the grounds, the views are the main attraction: Follow the little loop trail on the lake side of the castle for vistas down on Varenna's rooftops and the adjacent lakefront community of Pino. The castle itself is barren—a courtyard protecting an empty tower, where you can cross a drawbridge and climb 62 rickety wooden steps to earn 360 degrees of Lake Como panoramas.

Cost and Hours: €4, April-Sept Mon-Fri 10:00-18:00, Sat-Sun 10:00-19:00, July-Aug stays open one hour later, March and Oct closes one hour earlier, closed Nov-Feb and in bad weather, mobile 333-448-5975, www.castellodivezio.it, Nicola.

Falconry Shows: The castle hosts low-key falconry shows, usually around 15:30—but check the website or call in the morning for times.

Hiking Back Down: You can hike back the way you came or make a loop by continuing down to the east end of Varenna, on a steeper, narrower, less-manicured trail. From the castle gate, turn right and follow signs for *Varenna Scabium* and *Sentiero del Viandante*. You'll wander past some backyards and some scenic tennis courts, then start to gradually descend, popping out at the parking garage for the Hotel Eremo Gaudio. From here, head down to the right to walk back into Varenna, passing the entrances for both Villa Monastero and Villa Cipressi (described next) on your way to the main square.

Gardens

Two separate manicured lakeside gardens sit next door to each other just a short distance from the main square. First are the small but lush terraces of **Villa Cipressi;** just beyond are the more open grounds of **Villa Monastero,** which also admits visitors into the former residence of the De Marchi family, now a museum filled with overly ornate furnishings from the late 1800s. It's the handiest look inside one of the old villas that line the lakeshore, but the lack of information makes the place feel sterile. While the villas and gardens elsewhere on the lake are more magnificent (see "More Sights on Lake Como," later), these are a sufficient substitute if you're staying around Varenna.

Cost and Hours: Villa Cipressi—€4, May-Nov daily 8:00-20:00, closed Dec-April, www.hotelvillacipressi.it; Villa Monastero—gardens—€5, gardens and museum—€8; gardens open March-Oct daily 9:30-19:00, closed Nov-Feb; museum open March-Oct Fri-Sun 9:30-19:00, closed Mon-Thu—except open daily in Aug, closed Nov-Feb; bar in garden serves snacks, tel. 0341-295-450, www.villamonastero.eu.

Nearby: The **Sala De Marchi,** across the street from the Villa Monastero entrance, hosts a different exhibition each month through the summer. Ask at the TI or check the posters to see what's on.

Swimming

There are three spots to swim in Varenna: the free little beach behind the Hotel Royal Victoria off Piazza San Giorgio, the central lakefront area by Nilus Bar, and the *lido.* The *lido* is by far the best-equipped for swimmers. Just north of the boat dock, it's essentially a wide concrete slab with sand and a swimming area off an old boat ramp. It has showers, bathrooms, a restaurant, a bar, and lounge chairs and umbrellas for rent (entry-€2, tel. 0341-815-3700). Swimming by the boat dock is strictly forbidden for safety reasons.

Boat Tours

Taxi Boat Varenna organizes hour-long central lake tours (€30/person), plus a 2.5-hour version that adds a stop at Villa Balbianello (€55/person, includes a 1-hour guided villa tour). They also offer 50-minute romantic private tours (€150/couple). Ask Luca about his special 2.5-hour "Tour George." Book directly on the website (April-Oct only, mobile 349-229-0953, www.taxiboatvarenna.com, info@taxiboatvarenna.com). A similar company works out of Bellagio.

Hiking

The town of **Fiumelatte,** about a half-mile south of Varenna, was named for its "milky river." Promoted as the shortest river in Italy (at 800 feet), it runs—like most of the area's tourist industry—only from April through September (though even then it may be dry, depending on the weather). The *La Sorgente del Fiumelatte* brochure, available at Varenna's TI, lays out a walk from Varenna to the Fiumelatte, then to the castle, and back. It's a 30-minute hike to the source *(sorgente)* of the river (at Varenna's monastery, take the high road, drop into the tranquil and evocative cemetery, and climb steps to the wooded trail leading to the peaceful and refreshing cave from which the river spouts).

For a longer hike in the opposite direction with lake views, ask the TI about the **Wayfarers' Path** (hike one-way up the lake, about 2-2.5 hours, not quite as steep as Fiumelatte hike). You can return by train or boat from Bellano (check schedule before you go).

Cooking Course

Chef Moreno of the recommended Ristorante il Caminetto picks you up in Varenna, zips you up the mountain to his restaurant (experience Italian driving!), and then teaches you some basics of Italian cooking. Learn how to handcraft fresh pasta or prep regional specialties. Classes last about three hours, plus time to *mangiare*. People love the experience and find Moreno a charming teacher and host (€60 includes trip, lesson, recipes, and lunch complete with wine, cookies, and coffee; Mon, Tue, Thu, and Fri; 10:00 pickup from Varenna landing, return by 16:00, reservations mandatory, tel. 0341-815-127, www.ilcaminettoonline.com, info@ilcaminettoonline.com).

Sleeping in Varenna

Reservations are tight in August, snug May through October, and wide open most of the rest of the year. Many places close in winter. High-season prices are listed here; prices get soft off-season.

$$$ Hotel du Lac, filling a refined and modernized 19th-century villa, is the finest hotel in town. From its exclusive private perch on the point, it offers a quiet lakefront breakfast terrace; genteel public spaces; a friendly, professional staff; and 16 delightful rooms—all but three with lake views (ample standard Db-€198, bigger Db-€260, €20 less in April and late Oct, air-con, some rooms with elevator access, parking-€18/day, Via del Prestino 11, tel. 0341-830-238, www.albergodulac.com, info@albergodulac.com).

$$$ Albergo Milano, located right in the old town, is graciously run by Egidio and his Swiss wife, Bettina. Fusing the best of Italy with the best of Switzerland, this well-run, romantic hotel has eight comfortable rooms with extravagant views, balconies, or big terraces (Sb-€130, Db-€155-195 depending on view and terrace, extra bed-€35, €5/day cash discount, ceiling fans, no elevator; from the station, take main road to town and turn right at steep alley where sidewalk and guardrail break; Via XX Settembre 35, tel. 0341-830-298, www.varenna.net, hotelmilano@varenna.net). This place whispers *luna di miele*—honeymoon (see website for 3-night honeymoon deal). Nearby is **$$ Casa Rossa,** an annex with five comfortable rooms and one apartment that works well for families (same prices, breakfast served at main hotel). Their recommended Ristorante la Vista is worth considering for dinner.

Sleep Code

Abbreviations   1 = about $1.10, country code: 39)
S=Single, **D**=Double/Twin, **T**=Triple, **Q**=Quad, **b**=bathroom
Price Rankings
  $$$ Higher Priced—Most rooms €160 or more
  $$ Moderately Priced—Most rooms €110-160
  $ Lower Priced—Most rooms €110 or less
Unless otherwise noted, credit cards are accepted, breakfast is included, free Wi-Fi and/or a guest computer is generally available, and English is spoken. Many towns in Italy levy a hotel tax of €1.50-5 per person, per night (often collected in cash; usually not included in the rates I've quoted). Prices change; verify current rates online or by email. For the best prices, always book directly with the hotel.

$$$ Villa Cipressi is a sprawling, centuries-old lakeside mansion with 33 warmly outfitted, modern rooms. Its elegant but understated public spaces are often busy with wedding parties. Rooms without views face the street and can be noisy. The villa sits in a huge, quiet, terraced garden that nonguests pay to see (Sb-€160, nonview Db-€195, view Db-€220-230, extra bed-€70, ask for Rick Steves discount, all rooms have air-con or ceiling fans, elevator, garden access, Via IV Novembre 18, tel. 0341-830-113, www.hotelvillacipressi.it, info@hotelvillacipressi.it, Davide Dellera).

$$$ Hotel Royal Victoria, a central splurge facing the main square, has a classic, grand-hotel lobby, an inviting terrace with a swimming pool just above the lake, and 43 richly furnished rooms with modern amenities (Db-€240, lake view-€40 extra, extra bed-€60, air-con, elevator, pay Wi-Fi, parking-€20/day, Piazza San Giorgio 2, tel. 0341-815-111, www.royalvictoria.com, info@royalvictoria.com).

$$ Hotel Eremo Gaudio stands out with a commanding lake view high above Varenna. Once an orphanage, it became a hermitage run by the Catholic Church, and then—since 2000—a peaceful, modern hotel with awe-inspiring view balconies and a breakfast terrace. Thirteen bright, plain-but-comfy rooms climb up the main building, and 14 less dramatic but equally comfortable rooms huddle below at the foot of the funicular (prices with/without balcony—upper rooms: Sb-€115, Db-€136/€155; lower rooms: Sb-€115/€126, Db-€126/€141, Db with terrace-€155; all rooms have lake views, air-con in summer; from the station, it's a steep walk up hills and steps—taking a taxi is recommended; 5-minute walk from Varenna's main square at Via Roma 25, tel. 0341-815-301, www.hoteleremogaudiovarenna.it, eremogaudio@yahoo.it).

$$ Albergo del Sole rents eight simple, comfortable rooms above a restaurant right on the town square. Run by fun-loving Enzo, the hotel has no hint of a lake view, but may have rooms when others are full (Sb-€90, Db-€140, less off-season, family rooms, open all year, fans, hardwood floors, shiny bathrooms, elevator, Piazza San Giorgio 17, tel. 0341-815-218, www. albergodelsolevarenna.it, albergo.sole@virgilio.it).

$ Albergo Beretta, on the main road a block below the station, has 10 small, basic rooms, several with balconies (and street noise). Second-floor rooms are quietest. This place, above a coffee shop that doubles as the reception, feels homey but lacks any lakeside glamour (Sb-€65, Db-€75, larger room-€90, extra bed-€12, elevator, Wi-Fi in common areas, limited free parking—must reserve, Via per Esino 1, tel. 0341-830-132, hotelberetta@iol.it, Renato Brambilla).

$ Hotel Montecodeno, with 11 decent rooms and no views, is a functional concrete box along the main road. It's a five-minute walk from the train station and ferries (Sb-€80, Db-€105, extra bed-€20; book directly, stay 3 nights, show this book, and pay cash for 15 percent discount; air-con, no elevator, attached restaurant, Via della Croce 2, tel. 0341-830-123, mobile 340-356-7688, www.hotelmontecodeno.com, info@hotelmontecodeno.com, Marco Bartesaghi).

Eating in Varenna

Lavarello, a lake whitefish, is popular on menus. For something more adventurous, consider *missoltino*, which are salted little fish often served with pasta or local-style polenta (buckwheat is mixed in with the corn). As with Varenna's hotels, many of these restaurants close off-season (generally November through February or March).

DINING WITH A LAKE VIEW

Ristorante la Vista, at Albergo Milano, feels like a private hotel restaurant but also welcomes nonguests. On a balmy evening, their terrace overlooking the town and the lake is hard to beat. Egidio (or Egi—pronounced "edgy") and his staff give traditional cuisine a creative twist, and his selection is great for foodies with discerning tastes. While you can order à la carte, I'd go with his €38 three-course fixed-price dinner (€14-16 pastas, €17-22 *secondi;* Mon and Wed-Sat 19:00-22:00, closed Sun except June-Aug, closed Tue year-round; reservations required, Via XX Settembre 35, tel. 0341-830-298, www.varenna.net).

Ristorante la Contrada, with its terrace-side location, is run by the Villa Cipressi and takes advantage of the villa's elegant garden, trickling fountain, and lake view. Indoor seating glows with a warm and romantic air, and the garden is a delight on warm summer evenings. Fresh daily specialties and professional service make this a worthwhile splurge. However, weddings can crowd the place and distract from the service (€15-16 pastas, €19-23 *secondi*, daily 12:30-14:00 & 19:15-21:30, may close for weddings, Via IV Novembre 22, tel. 0341-830-113, www.hotelvillacipressi.it).

DINING WITHOUT A LAKE VIEW

Ristorante il Cavatappi, a classy little place on a quiet lane just off the town square, has only seven tables, so the cook-and-waiter team can connect personally with diners (€10-12 pastas, €15-20 *secondi*, Thu-Tue 12:00-14:00 & 18:30-21:30, closed Wed, reservations recommended for dinner, Via XX Settembre 10, tel. 0341-815-349, www.ilcavatappivarenna.it).

Osteria Quatro Pass is a welcoming bistro known for its homemade pasta, lake fish, and meat. It offers 14 candlelit tables under picturesque vaults, plus sidewalk seating. It has a fun energy that lets you know it's a popular spot (€12-18 pastas, €10-20 *secondi*, daily 12:00-14:00 & 18:30-22:00, closed Wed outside of peak season, Via XX Settembre 20, tel. 0341-815-091; Lilly serves while her son Giuseppe cooks).

Varenna Monamour's split-level interior, done up with stone and beams, feels contemporary but casual. Their menu has a nouvelle cuisine flair, and they pride themselves on specializing in seafood—not lake fish (€8-13 pastas, €10-19 *secondi*, daily 12:00-14:30 & 18:30-23:30, shorter hours and closed Tue off-season, Contrada Scoscesa 7, tel. 0341-814-016, www.varennamonamour.it).

EATING SIMPLY ON THE WATER

Along the waterfront in Varenna's old section are two simple eateries, both with great lakefront seating and relaxed (read: slow) service. Either of these is ideal for lingering over affordable (but forgettable) food in a stunning setting.

Nilus Bar, with a young waitstaff, serves crêpes, pizzas, big mixed salads, hot sandwiches, soup of the day, a few pastas, and cocktails (€7-12 meals, €5-6 sandwiches, Wed-Mon 12:00-22:30, closed Tue, bar open longer, tel. 0341-815-228, Fulvia and Giovanni).

Bar Il Molo, next door, is good for a casual meal on the harbor or a gelato with a view (€9-10 pizzas and pastas, €7-10 salads, €6 toasted sandwiches, daily 11:00-24:00, free Wi-Fi, tel. 0341-830-070). They also have a room full of gifty edibles for sale.

EATING SIMPLY WITHOUT A LAKE VIEW

Ristorante del Sole, facing the town square, serves respectable, well-priced meals and Neapolitan-style pizzas. This family-friendly restaurant provides a fun atmosphere, a cozy, walled-in garden in back, and tables on the square. Try their delicious and hearty *pizzocchere,* a handmade buckwheat pasta with melted cheese, potatoes, and greens (€7-10 pizzas, €7-14 pastas, €11-20 *secondi,* daily 11:00-16:00 & 18:30-late, closed Tue Nov-Feb, free Wi-Fi, Piazza San Giorgio 17, tel. 0341-815-218, www.albergodelsolevarenna.it).

High Above Town: **Ristorante il Caminetto** is a homey, backwoods mountain trattoria in Gittana, a tiny town in the hills above Varenna. Getting there entails a curvy 10-minute drive—they'll pick you up for free in Piazza San Giorgio, deliver you to the restaurant, and then dish up classic fare at small-town prices. Husband-and-wife team Moreno and Rossella take pride in their specialties, including grilled meats and risotto with porcini mushrooms and berries. This is a good place to set a price and trust your host to bring whatever's best (€28 three-course menu, wine and dessert extra, Thu-Tue 19:30-21:30, Sat-Sun also 12:30-14:30, closed Wed, reservations mandatory to confirm pickup from Varenna, Viale Progresso 4, tel. 0341-815-127, mobile 347-331-2238, www.ilcaminettoonline.com).

OTHER EATERIES

Pub l'Orso is the hotspot in town for wine or beer and a light meal. Oozing character, it's behind Hotel Olivedo in a renovated shed that used to be a joiner's workshop (closed Mon). The venerable **Vecchia Varenna** is the only classy restaurant actually on the harbor (old place with new management). And at **Hotel Olivedo,** a grand old hotel facing the ferry dock, you can eat in a classic dining hall.

Takeout Pizza: **Da Luigi Pizza da Re** bakes good €5-8 pies to take away, and delivers in the center for €2 extra (daily 10:30-14:30 & 17:00-21:00, closed Tue off-season, Via XX Settembre 7, mobile 334-543-9196).

Gelato: At **Gelateria Riva,** overlooking the water, you can get a cup or cone to go, then grab a pillowy seat on the bulkhead. Duilio is the only guy in town who prepares his gelato fresh every day. Try his *nocciola* (hazelnut) before making your choice. Ask the day before if you want to watch the gelato being made (daily 12:00-19:00, open later June-Sept).

Picnics: Varenna's two little grocery stores have all you need for a tasty balcony or breakwater picnic. The *salumeria* on the main square is best for meats, cheese, and bread; try their homemade salami (Tue-Sat 7:30-12:30 & 16:00-19:30, Sun-Mon 7:30-12:30 only, Via IV Novembre 2). The store just north of the main square by the pharmacy stocks fresh fruits, veggies, and a few essentials (daily 7:30-12:30, Tue-Sat also 16:00-19:30, Via Venini 6).

Varenna Connections

BY TRAIN

Before leaving Varenna, buy your tickets from the I Viaggi del Ti-vano travel agency in the station. (To avoid lines and stress at the station, you can also buy tickets in advance in the town center at the Barilott bar/tobacco shop just off the main square.) Stamp your ticket in the yellow machine at the station before boarding. If the office is closed and you can't buy tickets, win the sympathy of the conductor and buy your ticket as soon as you get on board for a small additional fee. (Find him before he finds you—or you'll likely be dinged with a €50 fine.)

Varenna to Milan: Trains from Varenna to Milano Centrale take about one hour and leave at :37 past most hours (with a few two-hour gaps in the schedule; confirm specific times at the station or online at www.trenitalia.com). Additional connections require a change in Lecco and an extra 30 minutes.

Varenna to Stresa (on Lake Maggiore): You'll have to take the train back to Milano Centrale, then connect from there to Stresa (3-4 hours).

Varenna to St. Moritz (Switzerland): Take the train from Varenna to Tirano (1 hour), where you'll have a layover before boarding the scenic Bernina Express train to St. Moritz (another 2.5 hours, 3 connections/day in summer, 1/day late Oct-early May, www.rhb.ch). A quicker, more frequent, but less scenic route is to take the train to Chiavenna (changing in Colico), then transfer to the bus, which takes you over the Maloja Pass to St. Moritz (5-6/day, 3.5 hours total). For times and tickets, stop by the I Viaggi del Tivano travel agency (see "Helpful Hints," earlier). Don't forget your passport for trips into Switzerland.

Bellagio

The self-proclaimed "Pearl of the Lake" is a classy combination of tidiness and Old World elegance. If you don't mind that "tramp in a palace" feeling, it's a fine place to shop for ties and umbrellas while surrounding yourself with the more adventurous posh travelers. Heavy curtains between the harborfront arcades create welcome shade and keep visitors and their poodles from sweating. Thriving yet still cute, Bellagio is a much more substantial town than Varenna. And as much as I'd like to disdain a town that gave its name to a Las Vegas casino, I gotta admit—Bellagio is pretty nice.

Orientation to Bellagio

TOURIST INFORMATION

The TI is at the passenger boat and hydrofoil dock (Mon-Sat 9:00-12:30 & 13:30-17:30, Sun 10:30-12:30 & 14:30-17:30, shorter hours Nov-March, tel. 031-950-204, www.bellagiolakecomo.com). The TI has free brochures for three well-crafted walking tours, varying from one to three hours, all of which explore the city and environs. They also sell a hiking map that shows four different hikes with a range of difficulty and duration.

ARRIVAL IN BELLAGIO

Bellagio is best reached by boat from Varenna or Como.

By Boat: Bellagio has two sets of docks a couple of hundred yards apart. (When you depart, be sure you're at the right dock—ask when you buy your ticket.)

By Car: Parking is difficult, but you can try for a spot near the lake or in the parking lot at the ferry dock. Spaces marked with white lines are always free, yellow lines are for residents only, and blue lines are pay-to-park (use the pay-and-display machines).

HELPFUL HINTS

Market: There's a lakeside market every third Wednesday of the month.

Laundry: La Lavandera is bright and new. Don't be discouraged if it looks closed; the lights come on automatically when you enter. Bring clothes in an easy-to-carry bag, as stairs and cobbles make it hard with wheeled luggage (€8.50/load, open daily 24 hours, Salita Carlo Grandi 21, tel. 339-410-6852).

Sights in Bellagio

Villa Serbelloni Park

If you need a destination, you can take a guided tour of this park, which overlooks the town. The villa itself, owned by the Rockefeller Foundation, is not open to the public.

Cost and Hours: €9, tours mid-March-Oct Tue-Sun at 11:00 and 15:30; no tours Mon, Nov-mid-March, or when rainy; 1.5 hours, first two-thirds of walk is uphill, show up at the little tour office in the medieval tower on Piazza della Chiesa 15 minutes before tour time to buy tickets, confirm time at office, tel. 031-951-555.

Strolling

Explore the steep-stepped lanes rising from the harborfront. While Johnnie Walker and jewelry sell best at lake level, the natives shop

up the hill. Piazza della Chiesa, near the top of town, has a worth-a-look church (with a golden altarpiece under glittering mosaics; pick up the English handout that describes its art).

North of Town: The de facto capital of the mid-lake region, Bellagio is located where the two legs of the lake split off to the south. For an easy break in a park with a great view, wander right on out to the crotch. Meander behind the rich and famous Hotel Villa Serbelloni, and walk 10 minutes up a concrete alley to **Punta Spartivento** ("Point that Divides the Wind"). You'll pop out to find a Renoir atmosphere complete with an inviting bar-restaurant (see "Eating in Bellagio," later), a tiny harbor, and a chance to sit on a park bench and gaze north past Menaggio, Varenna, and the end of the lake to the Swiss Alps.

South of Town: For another stroll, head south from the car-ferry dock down the tree-shaded promenade. Ten minutes later, you'll pass the town's concrete swimming area and then the pleasant **Villa Melzi Gardens.** This lakeside expanse of exotic plants, flowers, trees, and Neoclassical sculpture was assembled by the vice president of Napoleon's Italian Republic in the early 19th century. Although a bit pricey and not as elaborate as some of the lake's finer gardens, it has a pleasant, tree-shaded promenade for a lakefront stroll. At the entrance, pick up the map identifying both sculptures and plants (€6.50, April-Oct daily 9:30-18:30, closed Nov-March, mobile 339-457-3838, www.giardinidivillamelzi.it). About 15 minutes beyond the far end of the garden, you'll reach San Giovanni, with a pebbly public beach (no showers).

Boating and Water Sports

With a small stand at the boat docks, **Bellagio Water Limousine** (run by Australian Jennine and Italian Luca) offers tours and private service in their luxurious and powerful boat. Their basic 2.5-hour tour, guided by Luca, includes a fun hour at mid-lake, with a float-by of Richard Branson's villa, as well as a stop at Villa del Balbianello, where you'll take an English tour (€50, 10 percent discount if you reserve directly and bring this book, price includes entry and tour of villa, generally runs April-Oct Tue and Thu-Sun at 13:30 and also often at 11:00, different tours Mon and Wed, check blackboard for day's offerings or call mobile 338-524-4914, www.bellagiowaterlimousine.com, bellagiowaterlimousine@gmail.com).

Bellagio

LAKES

1. Hotel Florence
2. Hotel/Rist./Snack Bar Metropole
3. Hotel Centrale
4. Albergo Europa
5. Bellagio B&B (Apartments)
6. Bellagio B&B (Reception)
7. Il Borgo Apartments
8. To Giardini di Villa Melzi Apartments
9. The Florence Ristorante
10. Trattoria San Giacomo
11. Bilacus Ristorante & Aperitivo Et Al
12. Rist. Terrazza Barchetta
13. Enoteca Cava Turacciolo
14. Gelateria del Borgo
15. Groceries (2)
16. To La Punta Ristorante
17. Launderette
18. Villa Serbelloni Park Tickets
19. Bellagio Water-Limousine Lake Tours
20. To Bellagio Water Sports (Kayak Tours)

At **Bellagio Water Sports**, friendly Michele offers kayaking tours within a 10-minute walk of the town center. His popular two-hour tour (€35) covers the Bellagio coast, while his three-hour tour (€45) includes a stop at Villa Melzi. He also rents kayaks for those willing to go solo (no tours on Sun, weather-dependent late March and Oct, closed Nov-mid-March, located on Pescallo Bay near Hotel La Pergola at Via Sfondrati 1, mobile 340-394-9375, www.bellagiowatersports.com, info@bellagiowatersports.com).

Sleeping in Bellagio

This is a "boom or bust" lake resort, with high-season prices (those listed here) straight through from May to September, plus a brief shoulder season (with discounted prices) in April and from October to November. Bellagio closes down almost completely from December to February and is only half-open in March.

$$$ Hotel Florence has a prime lakefront setting in the center of town. The 150-year-old, family-run place features 30 rooms, hardwood floors, bold earth tones with splashes of bright colors, and a rich touch of Old World elegance (Sb-€125, Db-€150-220, Db suite-€250-320, prices depend on view and balcony, air-con in some rooms, elevator, Piazza Mazzini 46, tel. 031-950-342, www.hotelflorencebellagio.it, info@hotelflorencebellagio.it, run by the Austrian Ketzlar family).

$$$ Hotel Metropole, dominating Bellagio's waterfront between the ferry docks, is a grand old place with plush public spaces. Its modern rooms have all the comforts and classic flair. All of its 42 rooms have lake views, either side or full (Sb-€120, €140 with balcony; Db-€160, €200 with balcony, €230 with terrace; air-con, elevator, stunning roof terrace, Piazza Mazzini 1, tel. 031-950-409, www.albergometropole.it, info@albergometropole.it).

$$ Hotel Centrale, managed with pride and care by Giacomo Borelli, warmly welcomes its guests into a true-blue family operation: Signore Borelli's two sons help out, his mama painted the art, and grandpa crafted much of the Art Deco-era furniture. The 17 comfortable but dated rooms lack views, but the public spaces are generous (Sb-€110, Db-€130, €5/night discount with this book if you book directly with hotel, air-con, elevator, free calls to North America from reception, Salita Plinio 7, tel. 031-951-940, www.hc-bellagio.com, info@hc-bellagio.com).

$ Albergo Europa, run with low energy, is in a concrete annex behind a restaurant, away from the waterfront. Its nine basic rooms have no charm but get the job done (Db-€95, Tb-€115, no elevator, free parking, Via Roma 21, tel. 031-950-471, www.hoteleuropabellagio.it, info@hoteleuropabellagio.it, Marchesi family).

$ Bellagio B&B Apartments rents three units at the top of town, up the street from the *gelateria* (Db-€70, extra bed-€15, 2-night minimum, kitchens but no breakfast, reception a couple of blocks away at Salita Plinio 8, apartments at Salita Cavour 37, tel. 031-951-680, www.bellagiobedandbreakfast.com, info@bellagiobedandbreakfast.com). Owner Giulio also has five large apartments a 15-minute walk from Bellagio (toward Como, Db-€80-100 for 4 people, www.bellagioronchi.com).

$ Il Borgo Apartments offers seven efficient, modern units in the old center. Equipped with kitchenettes, these are a great deal for families or small groups. Easygoing Flavio is available for check-in daily 9:00-12:00, or by appointment (Db-€100, 2 bigger apartments for up to 6 people-€120, €5/night discount with this book if you book directly with hotel, cash preferred, no breakfast, 3-night minimum in peak season, 2-night minimum off-season, air-con, elevator, Salita Plinio 4, tel. 031-952-497, mobile 338-193-5559, www.borgoresidence.it, info@borgoresidence.it).

South of Town: **$ Giardini di Villa Melzi Apartments** features three modern doubles and three studios with kitchenettes in the little harbor of Loppia, about a 15-minute walk south of Bellagio. A free pass allows guests to take a shortcut to Bellagio through the Villa Melzi Gardens (Db-€100, extra bed-€50, cash only, no breakfast, usually 3-night minimum—ask, free parking, Via Melzi d'Eril 23, at the southern entrance to the gardens, tel. 339-221-4394, www.bellagiowelcome.com, info@bellagiowelcome.com, Ornella).

Eating in Bellagio

ON THE LAKEFRONT

The restaurants in these two recommended hotels offer wonderful lakeside tables and, considering the setting, acceptable prices.

Hotel Metropole's **Terrazzo Ristorante,** while a mediocre food value, has a full menu and is a relaxing delight with good service (€13-19 pastas, €17-25 *secondi*). **Hotel Metropole Snack Bar,** next to the restaurant, with good service in a great location, has simple €10-12 pastas and sandwiches and fine €9-12 salads (both are open long hours daily, but restaurant closes for midafternoon break, Piazza Mazzini 1, tel. 031-950-409).

The Florence is nicely situated under a trellis of flowers across from the Florence Hotel, away from the ferry fumes. This is a lovely perch for a drink or meal (€16 pastas, €25 *secondi*, simpler lunch menu of salads and lighter fare, April-Sept daily 12:00-14:30 & 19:00-22:00, bar open all day, tel. 031-950-342).

IN THE OLD TOWN, WITHOUT LAKE VIEWS

Trattoria San Giacomo is a high-energy place with traditional cuisine, such as *riso e filetto di pesce* (rice and perch fillet in butter and sage). It has seasonal specials and inviting €25 fixed-price meals (choose meat or fish) based on regional specialties. It offers fun seating on a steep, cobbled lane or tight seating inside (€8-9 pastas, €11-18 *secondi,* no cover, Mon and Wed-Thu 12:00-14:30 & 19:00-21:30, Fri-Sun open later midday and evenings, closed Tue, Salita Serbelloni 45, tel. 031-950-329, www.trattoriabellagio. it, Aurelio).

Across the street and sharing the same owner, **Bilacus Ristorante** has a brighter, more open dining room, a fine garden terrace, an emphasis on wine (including some top-quality vintages by the glass), and a menu with a bit more variety beyond local specials (€8-12 pastas, €12-18 *secondi*, Tue-Sun 11:30-15:00 & 18:30-22:00, closed Mon, Salita Serbelloni 32, tel. 031-950-480, www. bilacusbellagio.it).

Ristorante Terrazza Barchetta, set on a terrace with no lake view and bedecked with summery colors, puts a creative twist on regional favorites such as lake fish. Don't confuse it with the street-level bar-trattoria—head up the stairs to the second floor. Reservations are recommended (€11-18 pastas, €17-24 *secondi*, daily 12:00-14:30 & 19:00-22:30, Salita Mella 13, tel. 031-951-389, www. ristorantebarchetta.com).

OTHER OPTIONS

Wine Tasting: Step into the vaulted stone cellar of the funky **Enoteca Cava Turacciolo** to taste three regional wines with a sampling of cheeses, meats, and breads (€19/person with this book, April-Oct Thu-Tue 10:30-24:00, shorter hours Nov-Dec and March, closed Wed and Jan-Feb, Salita Genazzini 3, tel. 031-950-975, www.cavaturacciolo.it, Norberto and Rosy). **Aperitivo Et Al,** slick and jazzy, is a trendier wine bar (€17-26/three-glass tasting); it also offers mixed *salumi* and *formaggi* plates (€8-12), big fresh salads (€9-12), and light lunches. There's a great selection of wines by the glass (daily 11:30-24:00, closed Tue off-season, Wi-Fi, Salita Serbelloni 34, tel. 031-951-523).

Gelato: Residents agree that you won't find the best *gelateria* in town among the sundaes served on the waterfront. Instead, climb to the top of town to **Gelateria del Borgo** (Via Garibaldi 46, tel. 031-950-755, Stefania and Gianfranco).

Picnics: You'll find benches at the park, along the waterfront in town, and lining the promenade south of town. Two little groceries can make sandwiches and also sell a few prepared foods: the fancier **Butti Macelleria e Salumeria**, on the upper street near the *gelateria* (Tue-Sat 8:00-13:00 & 16:00-19:00, Sun 8:00-13:00, closed Mon, Via Garibaldi 42, tel. 031-950-333); and the simpler **Gastronomia Antichi Sapori,** on a cross street below the church (daily 7:30-19:30, Via Centrale 3, tel. 031-950-431).

Punta Spartivento: This dramatic natural park, a 10-minute walk north of town, is a great place for either a picnic or a meal at **La Punta Ristorante** (€13-15 pastas, €15-18 fish, €23-25 meat courses, March-Oct daily 12:00-14:30 & 19:00-22:00, bar open 14:30-19:00 for snacks only, tel. 031-951-888, www.ristorantelapunta.it).

More Sights on Lake Como

For the best one-day look at Lake Como, take my self-guided ferry tour to get your bearings, and hop off at the towns and villas of your choice. The two main villas worth considering (both described after the tour) are Villa Carlotta—with a sterile, museum-like interior and gorgeous, sprawling gardens—and Villa del Balbianello, a bit harder to reach but with a more striking setting, gardens that are more architectural than botanical, and a fascinating tour of the lived-in interior. If you have time, visit both—they're complementary. In this section, I also describe two other lake towns: Menaggio and Como, plus how to side-trip to Lugano in Switzerland.

▲▲Self-Guided Ferry Tour

The best simple day out is to take the *battello navetta* (mid-lake ferry) on its entire 50-minute Varenna-Bellagio-Villa Carlotta-

Tremezzo-Lenno route (generally departs Varenna at :23 past each hour, confirm times locally). On the return trip, hop off at any sights that interest you: Lenno (to see Villa del Balbianello), Villa Carlotta, and/ or Bellagio. This commentary describes what you'll see along the way, leaving from Varenna, though it's doable from Bellagio too.

Leaving Varenna: Looking back at Varenna from the lake, you'll see Vezio Castle rising above the town, with new Varenna on the left (bigger buildings and modern ferry dock), and old Varenna on the right (tighter, more colorful buildings). The big development high on the hillside is an ugly example of cronyism (without the mayor involved, this would never have happened). Under the castle is a grove of olives—reputedly the northernmost ones grown in Italy. Because the lake is protected from the north wind, exotic flowers grow well in the lake's many fine gardens. To the right of Varenna's castle are the town cemetery, a lift up to Hotel Eremo Gaudio (a former hermitage), and a spurt of water gushing out of the mountain just above lake level. This is the tiny Fiumelatte, Italy's shortest river.

• *On your way across to Bellagio, take a look around.*

Mid-Lake: The Swiss Alps rise to the north. Directly across the lake from Varenna is Menaggio, and just over the ridge from there are Lugano and the "Swiss Riviera." The winds alternate between north and south. In preindustrial times, traders harnessed the wind to sail up and down the lake. Notice the V-shaped, fjord-like terrain. Lake Como is glacier-cut. And, at more than 1,200 feet deep, it's Europe's deepest lake. You'll cruise past the Punta Spartivento, the bulbous point that literally "splits the wind," and where the two "legs" of the lake join (Lake Lecco is on the left/east, and Lake Como on the right).

• *Before long, you'll be...*

Approaching Bellagio: Survey the park at Punta Spartivento—it's a pleasant walk from town. Bellagio has three times the number

of hotel rooms as Varenna, as you can see upon approach. The town, with its strip of swanky hotels, is bookended by Villa Serbelloni (five stars) on the left, dominating the lakefront, and the sprawling Grand Hotel Bretagne (four stars) on the right. In the 19th century, aristocratic Russians hung out in the Serbelloni, and well-heeled English chose the Bretagne. These days, the Serbelloni is the second-most-luxurious hotel on the lake after Villa d'Este, while Bretagne is mired in a long renovation project.

• *Leaving Bellagio, about half the boats make a stop at **San Giovanni**, a small, nondescript lakefront community just down the shore from Bellagio. Whether your boat stops here or not, soon you'll head across the lake for a stop at...*

Villa Carlotta: Because of lake taxes and high maintenance costs, owners of once-elite villas have been forced to turn them into hotels or to open their doors to the paying public. Since 1927, this has been an example of the latter. One of the finest properties on the lake, Villa Carlotta has some good Neoclassical sculpture (including works by Canova) and one of the lake's lushest gardens (see listing below).

• *The shortest hop on this route (you could walk it in less than 10 minutes) takes you along to the town of...*

Tremezzo: As you leave the dock at Villa Carlotta, notice the Grand Hotel Tremezzo, with its striking Liberty-Style (Art Nouveau) facade and swimming pool floating on the lake. Above the town is a villa built in the 19th-century Romantic Age to resemble a medieval castle (next to the stub of a real one).

After the Tremezzo stop—and just before the Tremezzo church—you'll see a public park with a fountain and balustrade. When the road separated this land from its villa, its owners gave it to the community. Here the lake is dotted by a string of old villas with elegant landings and gated boathouses. Built in the days before motors, they are now too small for most modern lake boats.

Lenno: This pleasant resort town—with a long, arcing bay sheltering lots of little docks, and a generously shaded promenade—is the boat's last stop.

It's decision time: If you want to see the recommended **Villa del Balbianello,** hop off here. Return boats depart hourly; check the schedule before you set off. If you'd prefer to sail back to **Villa Carlotta, Bellagio,** or **Varenna,** you can probably stay put—this is the end of the line, so the boat's going to turn around and head back that way (but for some departures, you may be evicted and need to wait for the next boat).

▲Villa Carlotta

For gardens and flowers (its forte), this is the best of Lake Como's famed villas—especially in spring, when the many flowers are in bloom. For gardeners, it's worth ▲▲▲. I see the lakes as a break from Italy's art, but if you need a culture fix, Villa Carlotta also offers an elegant Neoclassical interior with a sculpture gallery, including works by Antonio Canova.

Cost and Hours: €9 includes villa/museum and gardens, daily April–mid-Oct 9:00-19:30, last ticket sold at 18:00, museum closes at 18:30, shorter hours last 2 weeks of March and mid-Oct-mid-Nov, closed mid-Nov-mid-March, tel. 034-440-405, www.villacarlotta.it.

Getting There: Villa Carlotta, at the southern end of the town of Tremezzo, has its own ferry dock (served by the *battello* passenger ferries). It's also less than a 10-minute walk from the Tremezzo and Cadenabbia docks (each served by a variety of boats). In a pinch, you can also use bus #C10 to zip along the lakefront to Lenno, near Villa del Balbianello (1-2/hour, buy ticket on bus, bus stop to the right as you exit Villa Carlotta).

Visiting the Villa: When buying your ticket, pick up the map that identifies the rooms in the house and the major plant groups in the gardens.

From the entrance, hike up the grand staircase and enter the **villa** itself. The main floor is filled with Neoclassical sculpture, including Antonio Canova's *Maddalena Penitente* and *Palamede* and works by his students (look for the impressive replica of Canova's famous *Love and Psyche Reclining*). There are also pieces by the great Danish sculptor Bertel Thorvaldsen. On the next floor up are generally well-presented special exhibits, and on the top floor are painstakingly appointed period rooms with elegant Empire Style furniture.

Then explore the main attraction, the **gardens**, which sprawl in both directions from the villa. To the south (toward Tremezzo) is the classical Old Garden. To the north, things get more interesting: pretty camellias, luscious azaleas, a maze of rhododendrons, a bamboo garden, and the gasp-worthy Valley of the Ferns—a lush jungle gorge with a river coursing through it.

▲▲Villa del Balbianello

The dreamiest villa on the lake perches on a romantic promontory near Lenno, overlooking Lake Como and facing Bellagio. Built at the end of the 18th century on the remains of an old Franciscan church, today the villa reflects the exotic vision of its last owner, explorer and mountaineer Guido Monzino, who died in 1988—leaving his villa and everything in it to the state. It's well worth paying extra to tour the interior to get to know Monzino, who led the first Italian expedition to climb Mount Everest in 1973. But the real masterpiece here is the terraced garden and elegant loggia, where the land fits the architecture and landscaping in a lovely way. This is a favorite choice for movie directors when they need a far-out villa to feature; this is where James Bond recovered from a particularly bruising experience in *Casino Royale,* and where Anakin first kissed Padmé (and later married her) in *Star Wars: Episode II—Attack of the Clones.*

Cost and Hours: Garden only— €8, garden with villa tour—€15, Thu-Sun and Tue 10:00-18:00, closed Mon and Wed and mid-Nov-mid-March, last entry to garden 45 minutes before closing, tel. 034-456-110, www. fondoambiente.it.

Tours: The only way inside the

villa is with an English tour. These depart at least hourly (more frequently with demand); the first tour is usually at 11:15 and the last at 16:30.

Getting There: It's at the end of a hilly point next to the town of Lenno. From the Lenno ferry dock, turn left and stroll around to the far end of the harbor (about 5 minutes). Here, you can either pay for a **speedboat shuttle** (€5.50 one-way, €7.50 round-trip, mobile 333-410-3854) or carry on by foot. If you choose to **walk**, continue past the boat dock and through the gate marked *Via del Balbianello*, where two options are clearly signposted in kilometers: a 20-minute, 1-kilometer (half-mile) hike (including some up and down), or a more challenging 45-minute, 2.5-kilometer (about 1 mile) huff over the top.

Visiting the Villa: Your visit includes two parts: the villa and the gardens.

Poke around the **gardens** while waiting for your villa tour to begin. On the Bellagio-facing side, you'll find a tranquil terrace

with sweeping lake views. Along the path, notice the circular stone shed. Originally used for refrigeration (they used ice from the mountains to keep things cool), today this shed houses the tomb of Guido Monzino. On the opposite side of the point, you'll find a terrace in front of the original Franciscan church (now a gift shop selling overpriced drinks). A WC is nearby, and just down the steps is the dock for the speed boat return to Lenno.

The 50-minute tour of the **villa** is as fascinating as its larger-than-life former owner. You'll tour the loggia (with a library and a study), then spend the rest of the time seeing 18 of the main building's 25 rooms. While finely decorated, these feel cozy, lived-in, and not too extravagant. Each one gives you a bit more insight into Monzino, from his personal living quarters, to his extensive collection of prehistoric artifacts from around the world, to the top-floor museum of his expeditions, with memorabilia from his North Pole and Mount Everest adventures. You'll see secret passages, learn why his furniture came with handles, and find out what's hiding behind the faux bookcase.

Menaggio

Menaggio—the third of the "big three" mid-lake towns (along with Varenna and Bellagio)—has more urban bulk than its neighbors, but visitors are charmed by its lovely lakefront park. Since many find Lake Como too dirty for swimming, consider spending time in Menaggio's fine public pool (look for the *lido*). This is

LAKES

the starting point for a few hikes. (Just a few decades ago, cigarette smugglers used these trails at night to sneak back into Italy from Switzerland with their tax-free booty.) The TI has information about mountain biking and catching the bus to trailheads on nearby Mount Grona. Ask for the free *Walking in the Province of Como* booklet, with information on 18 different walks detailing historical, artistic, and natural features (**TI** in Piazza Garibaldi open daily 9:00-12:30 & 14:30-18:00 except closed Sun Oct-mid-June and also Wed Nov-March, tel. 0344-32-924, www.menaggio.com).

Sleeping in Menaggio: **$ La Primula Youth Hostel** is a classic, old-school hostel, offering sailing lessons, Italian-language courses, cooking classes, kayak and bike rentals, and a great location on the lake, a two-minute walk from the ferry dock (Via IV Novembre 106, tel. 0344-32356, www.lakecomohostel.com).

Menaggio Connections: In addition to being connected to Varenna and Bellagio by all the regular boats, bus #C10 connects Menaggio to **Como town** in about an hour (1-2/hour). Menaggio is also a springboard for visiting Switzerland. Public bus #C12 departs about every hour or two from Piazza Roma for **Lugano** (around €10 round-trip, 1 hour, buy tickets at bus stop on Via Calvi). In summer, the yellow Palm Express bus runs once daily to **St. Moritz** (3.5 hours; off-season runs only weekends; reservations are required, www.postbus.ch)—remember to bring your passport.

Como Town

On the southwest tip of the lake, Como has a good, traffic-free old town, an interesting Gothic/Renaissance cathedral, a cable car up to a mountaintop viewpoint, and a pleasant lakefront with a promenade (**TI** closed Sun, tel. 031-269-712, www.lakecomo.it). It's an easy 10-minute walk from the boat dock to the train station (trains to Milan depart about twice per hour, 30-60 minutes).

All-Day Lugano Side-Trip

From Varenna or Bellagio, you can make a loop that lets you nip into Switzerland to see the elegant lake resort of Lugano, pass through the town of Como, and cruise a good part of Lake Como. Here's a good day plan (times are approximate—confirm schedules locally): about 9:30—ferry to Menaggio (15 minutes from Varenna); 10:30—bus to Lugano (1 hour, bring your passport);

11:30—explore Lugano; 16:00—train to Como (45 minutes); 17:00/18:00/19:00—fast hydrofoil from Como to Varenna (1 hour). For more information on Lugano, see www.ricksteves.com/lugano.

Lake Maggiore

Lake Maggiore is ringed by mountains, snowcapped in spring and fall, and lined with resort towns such as Stresa. Although Lake Maggiore lacks the cozy charm of Lake Como, a visit here may be worth the trouble for two islands, both with exotic gardens and lovely villas built by the Borromeo family.

The Borromeos—through many generations since 1630—lovingly turned their islands into magical retreats, with elaborate villas and fragrant gardens. Isola Bella has a palace and terraced garden; Isola Madre has a villa and sprawling English-style (more casual) garden. A third island, Isola Superiore (a.k.a. Isola Pescatori), is simply small, serene, and residential. The Borromeos, who made their money from trade and banking, enjoyed the arts—from paintings (hung in lavish abundance throughout the palace and villa) to plays (performed in an open-air theater on Isola Bella) and marionette shows (you'll see the puppets that once performed here). Although it's a characterless resort, the town of Stresa is a handy departure point for exploring Lake Maggiore's exotic garden islands.

Tourists flock here in May and June, when flowers are in bloom, and in September. Concerts held in scenic settings draw music lovers, particularly during the summer Stresa Festival (get details from Stresa TI). For fewer crowds, visit in April, July, August (when Italians prefer the Mediterranean beaches), or October. In winter, the snow-covered mountains (with resorts a 1.5-hour drive away) attract skiers.

PLANNING YOUR TIME

This region is best visited on a sunny day, when the mountains are clear, the lake is calm, and the heat of the sun brings out the scent of the blossoms. The two top islands for sightseeing are Isola Bella and Isola Madre (if tight on time, focus on Isola Bella). Isola Superiore has no sights, but is a peaceful place for lunch. You can stay the night in Stresa, but a day trip is sufficient for most.

Day Trip from Milan: Catch the one-hour, early train from Milan to the town of Stresa (usually at 8:25, which may require reservations, and likely also at 9:29—but check times carefully, as there's often a midmorning gap until 11:25). Upon arrival in Stresa, walk 10 minutes downhill to the boat dock, and catch a boat to Isola Madre. Work your way back to Isola Superiore for a lazy lunch, and then go on to Isola Bella for the afternoon, before returning to Stresa and back to Milan (trains leave about hourly—jot down your departure options on arrival in Stresa).

GETTING AROUND LAKE MAGGIORE

Boats link the islands and Stresa, running about twice hourly. Allow roughly 10 minutes between stops. Since short round-trip hops can add up fast (€6.80 for Isola Bella, €7.80 for Isola Superiore, €10 for Isola Madre, €12.40 for Villa Taranto), it's usually best to buy a **free circulation ticket,** which allows you to get off and on at intermediate stops between your departure and arrival ports (for instance, €13.80 includes Bella and Superiore, €16.90 covers all the islands, and €20.70 includes the islands and Villa Taranto).

Boats run daily April through September. The route: Stresa, Carciano/Lido (at the base of the cable car—but most boats skip this stop), Isola Bella, Isola Superiore, Baveno (lakeside town), Isola Madre, Pallanza, and Villa Taranto. This route is part of a longer one. To follow the boat schedule (free, available at boat docks and the TI), look at the Arona-Locarno timetable for trips from Stresa to the islands, and the Locarno-Arona timetable for the return trip to Stresa. Off-season, the boats cover a shorter route (public boat info: toll-free tel. 800-551-801, www.navigazionelaghi.it).

Buy boat tickets directly from the dock ticket booth under the gallery to the left of the TI. On the promenade to the boat dock, don't be fooled by the private taxi-boat drivers, most dressed in sailor outfits—they'll try to talk you into paying way too much for private tours on their smaller boats.

Sights on Lake Maggiore

Don't linger in Stresa—it's just a functional springboard. The main attractions are the islands and gardens.

STRESA

The town of Stresa—which means "thin stretch"—was named for the original strip of fishermen's huts that lined the shore. Today, grand old hotels run along that same shore.

Arrival in Stresa and Orientation: At the train station, ask for a free city map at the newsstand (to the far right of the tracks as you exit the train). To get downtown, exit right from the station and take your first left (on Viale Duchessa di Genova). This takes you straight down to the lake (once you're there, the boat dock is about four blocks to your right; ask for boat schedule at ticket window). The helpful **TI,** located to the right of the ticket window at the boat dock, has free maps and boat schedules (March-Oct daily 10:00-12:30 & 15:00-18:30, off-season closed Sat afternoon and all day Sun, Piazza Marconi 16, tel. 0323-30150, www.stresaturismo.it). Taxis charge a fixed rate of €8-9 for even the shortest ride in town.

Visiting Stresa: The **old town**—basically a traffic-free touristy shopping mall—is just a few blocks deep, stretching inland from the main boat dock. Stresa's stately 19th-century lakeside hotels date back to the days when this town was on the Grand Tour circuit.

In any Romantic Age resort like Stresa, hotels had names designed to appeal to Victorian aristocrats...like Regina Palace (rather than Palazzo), Astoria, Bristol, and Victoria.

The **Grand Hotel des Iles Borromees** was the first (built in 1862). In 1918, 19-year-old Ernest Hemingway—wounded in Slovenia as an ambulance driver for the Italian Red Cross—was taken to Stresa's Grand Hotel des Iles Borromees, which served, like its regal neighbors, as an infirmary during World War I. Hemingway returned to the same hotel in 1948, stayed in the same room (#205, now called the "Hemingway suite"—you can stay there for a couple of thousand dollars a night), and signed the guest book as "an old client." Another "old client" was Winston Churchill, who honeymooned here.

A fine waterfront promenade leads past the venerable old hotels to the Lido, with the Carciano boat dock and the **Stresa-Alpino-Mottarone cable car.** This cable car takes you up—in two stages and a 20-minute ride—to the top of Mount Mottarone (€19 round-trip to the top, €11.50 one-way, daily 9:30-17:40 in summer, shorter hours in winter, 2-3/hour, bar midway up, tel. 0323-30295, www.stresa-mottarone.it). From the top (about 5,000 feet), you get great panoramic views of neighboring peaks and, by taking a short

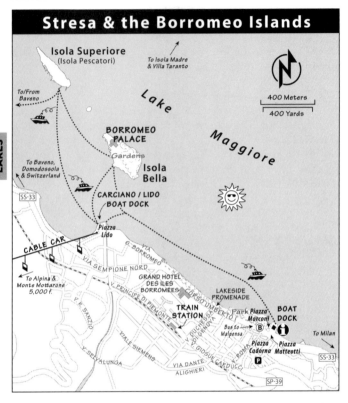

hike, a bird's-eye view of the small, neighboring Lake Orta (described later).

Halfway up the cable-car line are the **Alpine Gardens,** which come with fine lake views and picnic spots, but these gardens can't compare with what you'll see on the islands. To visit the gardens, get off at the midway Alpino stop and walk 10 minutes (turn left as you leave; €4, April-Oct daily 9:30-18:00, closed Nov-March). If you plan to hike down, pick up the *Trekking* map from the TI and allow four hours from the top of Mount Mottarone, or two hours from the Alpine Gardens (mountain biking also possible—ask at TI).

Sleeping in Stresa: Because Stresa's town generally lacks appeal, I'd day-trip from Milan. But if you'd like to stay, here are some options: **Hotel Saini Meublè** is a small, homey, affordable choice in the old town center (www.hotelsaini.it); **Hotel Milan Speranza Au Lac** is a big, group-oriented hotel facing the boat dock (www.milansperanza.it); and **Hotel Moderno** is a midsize, midrange option in the old town (www.hms.it).

Eating in Stresa: The main square, **Piazza Cadorna,** is one big tourist trap, yet it does have a certain charm. (At night, it seems anyone who claims to be a musician can get a gig singing for diners.) For a (slightly) less touristy alternative, seek out one of these options: **Osteria degli Amici**, tucked away under a vine trellis on a forgotten square a couple of blocks beyond Piazza Cadorna (Via Bolongaro 33); **La Botte,** with an old-school diner vibe on the main street between the port and the square (Via Mazzini 6); or **Il Clandestino,** a fancier, romantic, modern splurge specializing in fish (Via Rosmini 5).

ISLANDS AND GARDENS
▲▲Isola Bella

This island, nearest Stresa, has a formal garden and a fancy Baroque palace. Looking like a stepped pyramid from the water,

the island was named by Charles Borromeo (sponsor of Milan's Duomo) for his wife, Isabella. The island itself is touristy, with a gauntlet of souvenir stands and a corral of restaurants. A few back streets provide evidence that people actually live here. While the Borromeo family now lives in Milan, they spend a few weeks on Isola Bella each summer (when their blue-and-red family flag flies from the top of the garden).

Cost and Hours: Palace and garden-€15, €20.50 combo-ticket includes the villa at Isola Madre, daily late-March-late-Oct 9:00-18:00, shorter hours for palace's picture gallery, closed late-Oct-late-March, no photos in villa, tel. 0323-30556, www.borromeoturismo.it.

Tours: A fine €3 audioguide describes the palace, which also has posted English descriptions. A €1.50 booklet explains the gardens.

Services: A WC is located halfway through your visit, where you leave the villa and enter the gardens.

Eating: Several restaurants cluster between the boat docks and the villa. Picnicking is not allowed in the garden, but you can picnic in the pebbly park at the point of the island, beyond the villa (free and open to the public).

Visiting the Island: There are two docks on this island, one for each direction. It's a short walk from the boat to the hulking villa (turn left from the dock; on the way, you'll pass a public WC). Once inside, your visit is a one-way tour, starting with the palace and finishing with the garden. (There's no way to see the garden without the palace.)

In the lavishly decorated Baroque **palace,** stairs lead up under stucco crests of Italy's top families (balls signify the Medici, bees mean the Barberini, and a unicorn symbolizes the Borromeos' motto: Humility). You'll loop through the picture gallery, containing 130 beautifully restored 16th-century paintings from the Borromeo family's private collection, hung wall to ceiling in several cramped rooms. Then you'll get a peek at the canopied bed chambers and ogle the ornate throne room. Continue through the dining room, with a portrait of the first Borromeo, and into a richly stuccoed grand hall, with an 80-foot-high dome and featuring an 18th-century model of the villa, including a grand water entry that never materialized.

Next comes the music room, the site of the 1935 Stresa Conference, in which Mussolini met with British and French diplomats in a united attempt to scare Germany out of starting World War II. Look for a copy of the treaty with Mussolini's signature on the wall next to the exit. Unfortunately, the "Stresa Front" soon fizzled when Mussolini attacked Ethiopia and joined forces with Hitler.

Napoleon's bedroom comes with an engraving that depicts his 1797 visit (Napoleon is on a bench with his wife and sister enjoying festivities in his honor). Continue through several more opulent halls, many of which display souvenirs and gifts that the Borromeo family picked up over the generations.

Downstairs, many of the famous Borromeo marionettes are on display. (A larger collection is on Isola Madre.) The 18th-century, multiroom grotto, decorated from ceiling to floor with shell motifs and black-and-white stones, still serves its original function of providing a cool refuge from Italy's heat. The dreamy marble statues are by Gaetano Monti, a student of Antonio Canova. Climbing out of the basement, look up at the unique, cantilevered, spiral stairs; they're from a 16th-century fortress that predates this building.

Pass through the mirrored corridor and follow the route through more rooms until you come to the ornate hall of 16th-century Flemish tapestries. This leads to the finale of this island visit: the beautiful **garden,** complete with Chinese white peacocks, which give it an exotic splash. (Before continuing to the garden, consider heading up the stairs near the WC to stroll through Elisa's Greenhouse, named for Napoleon's sister and home to tropical plants.)

From the palace, head straight up the stairs into the main part of the garden. Baroque—which is exactly what you see here—is all about controlling nature. The centerpiece is a pyramid-shaped outdoor grotto, crowned by the Borromeo family unicorn. Up the stairs and behind this fanciful structure is a vast terrace with views over the lower gardens and Stresa. Back downstairs, follow the signs (hidden in the bushes) to the café and bookshop, which anchor the far points of the island, to see the terraces behind the "pyramid." Finally, follow *exit* signs to pop out a side gate at the top of a twisty, stepped lane back through town to the boat docks.

▲Isola Superiore (Pescatori)

This sleepy island—home to 35 families—is the smallest and most residential of the three. It has a few good fish restaurants, ample pizza-by-the-slice take-out joints, picnic benches, views, and, blissfully, nothing much to do—all under arbors of wisteria. Simply stroll the narrow, cobbled lanes, or relax at the long, skinny, pebbly park/beach at the tip of the island. A delight for photographers and painters, the island is never really crowded, except at lunchtime.

▲Isola Madre

Don't come to this island unless you intend to tour the sight, because that's all there is: an interesting furnished villa and a lovely garden filled with exotic birds and plants.

Cost and Hours: Villa and garden-€12, €20.50 combo-ticket includes Isola Bella, late-March-late-Oct daily 9:00-18:00, closed late-Oct-late-March, no photos in villa, tel. 0323-31261, www. borromeoturismo.it.

Information: The villa has a few sparse English descriptions. Garden lovers can invest €1.50 in a booklet about the plantings.

Services: A WC is next to the chapel. You'll also find a café/bookshop (selling basic sandwiches) just outside the villa. While eating is best on Isola Superiore, Isola Madre has one real restaurant, **La Piratera Ristorante Bar,** which owns a big, beautiful terrace over the lake. You'll run into this immediately after leaving the villa/garden complex (€24 fixed-price tourist meal, daily 8:00-18:00, sit-down meals 12:00-15:30, simple sandwiches and slices of pizza to go anytime, picnic at rocky beach a minute's walk from restaurant, just to your right as you exit the gardens, tel. 0323-31171).

Visiting the Island: Visiting is a one-way affair. From the boat dock, walk up the stairs to the ticket desk for the villa. Then, once through the gate, take the level path to the right to loop around the gardens and end at the villa (*ingresso al giardino* signs). Or, if you're in a rush, take the stairs to the left instead to go straight to the villa.

First you'll circle all the way around the **gardens.** Eight gardeners (with the help of water continually pumped from the lake) keep this English-style garden paradise lush. It's a joy, even for those bored by flowers and foliage. You'll see trees from around the world, and an exotic bird menagerie with golden and silver pheasants and Chinese peacocks. (You'll see and hear them roaming wild; also look for the bird cages partway up the main staircase to the villa, on the left.)

In front of the villa, a once-magnificent **Himalayan cypress tree** paints your world a streaky green. The 150-year-old tree, knocked down by a tornado in 2006 but successfully saved, is an attraction in its own right, with steel guy-wires now anchoring it firmly in place.

The 16th-century **villa** is the first of the Borromeo palaces. A century older than the Isola Bella villa, it's dark, somber, and dates from the Renaissance. The clever angled hinges keep the doors from flapping in the lake breeze. The family's huge collection of dolls, marionettes, and exquisite 17th-century marionette theater sets—painted by a famous La Scala opera set designer—fills several rooms. A corner room is painted to take you into an 18th-century Venetian Rococo sitting room under a floral greenhouse.

Some of the garden's best flowers are in view immediately after leaving the villa. Walk down the stairs to the terrace in front of the chapel, with WCs tucked around the left side. Stairs lead directly down to the boat dock from here. Or you can loop past the villa to exit at the far end, just above La Piratera restaurant. From there, you can walk through the shop to reach a terrace path that leads you back to the boat dock.

Villa Taranto Botanical Gardens

Garden lovers will enjoy this large landscaped park, located on the mainland across the lake from Stresa. Although it's the most sprawling garden in the area, and enjoyable for a stroll in a park, it's a bit underwhelming. The gardens are a Scotsman's labor of love. Starting in the 1930s, Neil McEacharn created this garden of delights—bringing in thousands of plants from all over the world—and here he stays, in the small mausoleum. The park's highlight is a terraced garden with a series of cascading pools. Villa Taranto is directly across the street from the boat dock.

Cost and Hours: €10, daily mid-March-Sept 8:30-18:30, Oct 9:00-16:00, closed Nov-mid-March, tel. 0323-404-555, www.villataranto.it.

Getting There: It's two stops (about 15 minutes) past Isola Madre. On the way, you'll pass a scenic promontory speckled with villas. Note that only about half of the lake boats stop here, which means an hour between return departures—check schedules carefully.

DAY TRIP FROM STRESA
▲Lake Orta

Just on the other side of Mount Mottarone is the small lake of Orta. The lake's main town, Orta San Giulio, has a beautiful lakeside

piazza ringed by picturesque buildings. The piazza faces the lake with a view of Isola San Giulio. Taxi boats (€4 round-trip) make the five-minute trip throughout the day. The island is worth a look for the Church of San Giulio and the circular "path of silence," which takes about 10 minutes. In peak season, Orta is anything but

silent, but off-season or early or late in the day, this place is full of peace and magic (TI open Sat-Sun 9:30-17:30, closed Mon-Fri, on Via Panoramica next to the parking lot downhill from the train station, tel. 0322-905-163).

Getting There: The train ride from Stresa to Orta-Miasino (a short walk from the lakeside piazza) takes 1.5-2 hours and requires a change or two (5/day). Public buses from Stresa's Piazza Marconi to Orta depart from near the TI (around €9 round-trip, about 1 hour, 2-3/day mid-June-mid-Sept, confirm schedule at TI or at www.safduemila.com).

LAKES

PRACTICALITIES

This section covers just the basics on traveling in Italy (for much more information, see *Rick Steves Italy*). You'll find free advice on specific topics at www.ricksteves.com/tips.

MONEY

Italy uses the euro currency: 1 euro (€) = about $1.10. To convert prices in euros to dollars, add about 10 percent: €20 = about $22, €50 = about $55. (Check www.oanda.com for the latest exchange rates.)

The standard way for travelers to get euros is to withdraw money from ATMs (which locals call a *bancomat*) using a debit or credit card, ideally with a Visa or MasterCard logo. Before departing, call your bank or credit-card company: Confirm that your card(s) will work overseas, ask about international transaction fees, and alert them that you'll be making withdrawals in Europe. Also ask for the PIN number for your credit card in case it'll help you use Europe's "chip-and-PIN" payment machines (see below); allow time for your bank to mail your PIN to you. To keep your valuables safe while traveling, wear a money belt.

Dealing with "Chip and PIN": Much of Europe (including Italy) is adopting a "chip-and-PIN" system for credit cards, and some merchants rely on it exclusively. European chip-and-PIN cards are embedded with an electronic chip, in addition to the magnetic stripe used on our American-style cards. This means that your credit (and debit) card might not work at payment machines, such as those at train and subway stations, toll roads, parking garages, luggage lockers, and gas pumps. Major US banks are beginning to offer credit cards with chips, but many of these are chip-and-signature cards, for which your signature (not your PIN) verifies your identity. In Europe, these cards should work for live transactions and at most payment machines, but probably won't work for offline transactions such as at unattended gas pumps. If a payment machine won't take your card, look for a machine that takes cash or see if there's a cashier nearby who can manually process your transaction. Often the easiest solution is to pay for your purchases with cash you've withdrawn from an ATM using your debit card (Europe's ATMs still accept magnetic-stripe cards).

Dynamic Currency Conversion: If merchants or hoteliers offer to convert your purchase price into dollars (called dynamic currency conversion, or DCC), refuse this "service." You'll pay more in fees for the expensive convenience of seeing your charge in dollars. If an ATM offers to "lock in" or "guarantee" your conversion rate, choose "proceed without conversion." Other prompts might state, "You can be charged in dollars: Press YES for dollars, NO for euros." Always choose the local currency.

STAYING CONNECTED

Smart travelers call ahead or go online to double-check tourist information, learn the latest on sights (special events, tour schedules, and so on), book tickets and tours, make reservations, reconfirm hotels, and research transportation connections.

To call Italy from the US or Canada: Dial 011-39 and then the local number. (The 011 is our international access code, and 39 is Italy's country code.)

To call Italy from a European country: Dial 00-39 followed by the local number. (The 00 is Europe's international access code.)

To call within Italy: Just dial the local number.

To call from Italy to another country: Dial 00 followed by the country code (for example, 1 for the US or Canada), then the area code and number. If you're calling European countries whose phone numbers begin with 0, you'll usually omit that 0 when you dial.

Tips: Traveling with a mobile phone—whether an American one that works in Italy, or a European one you buy when you arrive—is handy, but can be pricey. Consider getting an international plan; most providers offer a global calling plan that cuts the per-minute cost of phone calls and texts, and a flat-fee data plan.

Use Wi-Fi whenever possible. Most hotels and many cafés offer free Wi-Fi, and you'll likely also find it at tourist information offices, major museums, and public-transit hubs. With Wi-Fi you can use your smartphone to make free or inexpensive domestic and international calls by taking advantage of a calling app such as Skype, FaceTime, or Google+ Hangouts. When you can't find Wi-Fi, you can use your cellular network to connect to the Internet, text, or make voice calls. When you're done, avoid further charges by manually switching off "data roaming" or "cellular data."

It's possible to stay connected without a mobile phone. To make cheap international calls from any phone (even your hotel-room

From:	rick@ricksteves.com
Sent:	Today
To:	info@hotelcentral.com
Subject:	Reservation request for 19-22 July

Dear Hotel Central,

I would like to reserve a double room for 2 people for 3 nights, arriving 19 July and departing 22 July. If possible, I would like a quiet room with a bathroom inside the room.

Please let me know if you have a room available and the price.

Thank you!
Rick Steves

phone), you can buy an international phone card in Italy. These work with a scratch-to-reveal PIN code, allow you to call home to the US for pennies a minute, and also work for domestic calls. Calling from your hotel-room phone without using an international phone card is usually expensive. Though they are disappearing in Italy, you can still find public pay phones in post offices and train stations. For more on phoning, see www.ricksteves.com/phoning.

MAKING HOTEL RESERVATIONS

I recommend reserving rooms in advance, particularly during peak season. For the best rates, book directly with the hotel using their official website (not a booking agency's site). If there's no secure reservation form, or for complicated requests, send an email with the following information: number and type of rooms; number of nights; arrival date; departure date; and any special requests. (For a sample email, see the sidebar.) Use the European style for writing dates: day/month/year. Hoteliers typically ask for your credit-card number as a deposit.

Some hotels are willing to deal to attract guests—try emailing several to ask their best price. In general, hotel prices can soften if you do any of the following: offer to pay cash, stay at least three nights, or travel off-season. You can also try asking for a cheaper room or a discount.

While most taxes are included in the price, a variable city tax of €1.50-5/person per night is often added to hotel bills in Italy (and is not included in the prices in this book). Some hoteliers will ask to collect the city tax in cash to make their bookkeeping and accounting simpler.

EATING

Italy offers a wide array of eateries. A *ristorante* is a formal restaurant, while a *trattoria* or *osteria* is usually more traditional and simpler (but can still be pricey). Italian "bars" are not taverns, but small cafés selling sandwiches, coffee, and other drinks. An *enoteca* is a wine bar with snacks and light meals. Take-away food from pizza shops and delis (*rosticcería*) makes an easy picnic.

Italians eat dinner a bit later than we do; better restaurants start serving around 19:00. A full meal consists of an appetizer (antipasto), a first course (*primo piatto*, pasta, rice, or soup), and a second course (*secondo piatto*, expensive meat and fish/seafood dishes). Vegetables *(verdure)* may come with the *secondo*, but more often must be ordered separately as a side dish (*contorno*). Desserts (*dolci*) can be very tempting. The euros can add up in a hurry, but you don't have to order each course. My approach is to mix antipasti and *primi piatti* family-style with my dinner partners (skipping *secondi*). Or, for a basic value, look for a *menù del giorno*, a three- or four-course, fixed-price meal deal (avoid the cheapest ones, often called a *menù turistico*).

Good service is relaxed (slow to an American). You won't get the bill until you ask for it: *"Il conto?"* Most restaurants include a service charge in their prices (check the menu for *servizio incluso*—generally around 10 percent). You can add on a tip, if you choose, by including a euro or two for each person in your party. If you order at a counter rather than from waitstaff, there's no need to tip. Many (but not all) restaurants in Italy add a cover charge *(coperto)* of €1-3.50 per person to your bill.

At bars and cafés, getting a drink while standing at the bar (*banco*) is cheaper than drinking it at a table *(tavolo)* or sitting outside *(terrazza)*. This tiered pricing system is clearly posted on the wall. Sometimes you'll pay at a cash register, then take the receipt to another counter to claim your drink.

TRANSPORTATION

By Train: In Italy, most travelers find it's cheapest simply to buy train tickets as they go. To see if a railpass could save you money, check www.ricksteves.com/rail. To research train schedules, visit Germany's excellent all-Europe website, www.bahn.com, or Italy's www.trenitalia.com. A private company called Italo also runs fast trains on major routes in Italy; see www.italotreno.it.

You can buy tickets at train stations (at the ticket window or at machines with English instructions) or from travel agencies. Before boarding the train, you must validate your train documents by stamping them in the machine near the platform (usually marked *convalida biglietti* or *vidimazione*). Strikes *(sciopero)* are common and generally announced in advance (but a few sporadic trains still run—ask around).

By Car: It's cheaper to arrange most car rentals from the US. For tips on your insurance options, see www.ricksteves.com/

cdw, and for route planning, consult www.viamichelin.com. Theft insurance is mandatory in Italy ($15-20/day). In Italy, most car-rental companies' rates automatically include Collision Damage Waiver (CDW) coverage. Even if you try to decline CDW when you reserve your Italian car, you may find when you show up at the counter that you must buy it after all.

Bring your driver's license. You're also technically required to have an International Driving Permit (sold at your local AAA office for $15 plus the cost of two passport-type photos; see www.aaa.com).

Italy's superhighway *(autostrada)* system is slick and speedy, but you'll pay a toll. Be warned that car traffic is restricted in many city centers—don't drive or park in any area that has a sign reading *Zona Traffico Limitato* (*ZTL*, often shown above a red circle)...or you might be mailed a ticket later.

Italians love to tailgate; otherwise, local road etiquette is similar to that in the US. Ask your car-rental company for details, or check the US State Department website (www.travel.state.gov, click on "International Travel," then specify your country of choice and click "Traffic Safety and Road Conditions").

A car is a worthless headache in cities—park it safely (get tips from your hotelier). As break-ins are common, be sure all of your valuables are out of sight and locked in the trunk, or even better, with you or in your hotel room.

HELPFUL HINTS

Emergency Help: For English-speaking **police** help, dial 113. To summon an **ambulance**, call 118. For passport problems, call the **US Embassy** (in Rome, 24-hour line—tel. 06-46741) or **US Consulates** (Milan—tel. 02-290-351, Florence—tel. 055-266-951, Naples—tel. 081-583-8111); or the **Canadian Embassy** (in Rome, tel. 06-854-442-911). If you have a minor illness, do as the locals do and go to a pharmacist for advice. Or ask at your hotel for help—they'll know of the nearest medical and emergency services. For other concerns, get advice from your hotelier.

Theft or Loss: Italy has particularly hardworking pickpock-ets—wear a money belt. Assume beggars are pickpockets and any scuffle is simply a distraction by a team of thieves. If you stop for any commotion or show, put your hands in your pockets before someone else does.

To replace a passport, you'll need to go in person to an embassy or consulate (see above). Cancel and replace your credit and debit cards by calling these 24-hour US numbers collect: Visa—tel. 303/967-1096, MasterCard—tel. 636/722-7111, American Express—tel. 336/393-1111. In Italy, to make a collect call to the US, dial 800-172-444; press zero or stay on the line for an operator.

File a police report either on the spot or within a day or two; you'll need it to submit an insurance claim for lost or stolen railpasses or electronics, and it can help with replacing your passport or credit and debit cards. Precautionary measures can minimize the effects of loss—back up your digital photos and other files frequently. For more information, see www.ricksteves.com/help.

Time: Italy uses the 24-hour clock. It's the same through 12:00 noon, then keep going: 13:00, 14:00, and so on. Italy, like most of continental Europe, is six/nine hours ahead of the East/West Coasts of the US.

Business Hours: Many businesses have now adopted the government's recommended 8:00 to 14:00 workday (although in tourist areas, shops are open longer). Still, expect small towns and villages to be more or less shut tight during the midafternoon. Stores are also usually closed on Sunday, and often on Monday.

Sights: Opening and closing hours of sights can change unexpectedly; confirm the latest times with the local tourist information office or its website. Some major churches enforce a modest dress code (no bare shoulders or shorts) for everyone, even children.

Holidays and Festivals: Italy celebrates many holidays, which can close sights and attract crowds (book hotel rooms ahead). For information on holidays and festivals, check Italy's website: www.italia.it. For a simple list showing major—though not all—events, see www.ricksteves.com/festivals.

Numbers and Stumblers: What Americans call the second floor of a building is the first floor in Europe. Europeans write dates as day/month/year, so Christmas 2016 is 25/12/16. Commas are decimal points and vice versa—a dollar and a half is 1,50, and there are 5.280 feet in a mile. Italy uses the metric system: A kilogram is 2.2 pounds; a liter is about a quart; and a kilometer is six-tenths of a mile.

RESOURCES FROM RICK STEVES

This Snapshot guide is excerpted from my latest edition of *Rick Steves Italy*, which is one of more than 30 titles in my series of guidebooks on European travel. I also produce a public television series, *Rick Steves' Europe*, and a public radio show, *Travel with Rick Steves*. My website, www.ricksteves.com, offers free travel information, a forum for travelers' comments, guidebook updates, my travel blog, an online travel store, and information on European railpasses and our tours of Europe. If you're bringing a mobile device on your trip, you can download my free Rick Steves Audio Europe app, featuring podcasts of my radio shows, audio tours of major sights in Europe, and travel interviews about Italy. You can get Rick Steves Audio Europe via Apple's App Store, Google Play, or the Amazon Appstore. For more information, see www.

ricksteves.com/audioeurope. You can also follow me on Facebook and Twitter.

ADDITIONAL RESOURCES
Tourist Information: www.italia.it
Passports and Red Tape: www.travel.state.gov
Packing List: www.ricksteves.com/packing
Travel Insurance: www.ricksteves.com/insurance
Cheap Flights: www.kayak.com
Airplane Carry-on Restrictions: www.tsa.gov
Updates for This Book: www.ricksteves.com/update

How Was Your Trip?
If you'd like to share your tips, concerns, and discoveries after using this book, please fill out the survey at www.ricksteves.com/feedback. Thanks in advance—it helps a lot.

Italian Survival Phrases

English	Italian	Pronunciation
Good day.	*Buon giorno.*	bwohn **jor**-noh
Do you speak English?	*Parla inglese?*	**par**-lah een-**glay**-zay
Yes. / No.	*Sì. / No.*	see / noh
I (don't) understand.	*(Non) capisco.*	(nohn) kah-**pees**-koh
Please.	*Per favore.*	pehr fah-**voh**-ray
Thank you.	*Grazie.*	**graht**-seeay
You're welcome.	*Prego.*	**pray**-go
I'm sorry.	*Mi dispiace.*	mee dee-spee**ah**-chay
Excuse me.	*Mi scusi.*	mee **skoo**-zee
(No) problem.	*(Non) c'è un problema.*	(nohn) cheh oon proh-**blay**-mah
Good.	*Va bene.*	vah **behn**-ay
Goodbye.	*Arrivederci.*	ah-ree-vay-**dehr**-chee
one / two	*uno / due*	**oo**-noh / **doo**-ay
three / four	*tre / quattro*	tray / **kwah**-troh
five / six	*cinque / sei*	**cheeng**-kway / **seh**ee
seven / eight	*sette / otto*	**seht**-tay / **ot**-toh
nine / ten	*nove / dieci*	**nov**-ay / dee**eay**-chee
How much is it?	*Quanto costa?*	**kwahn**-toh **kos**-tah
Write it?	*Me lo scrive?*	may loh **skree**-vay
Is it free?	*È gratis?*	eh **grah**-tees
Is it included?	*È incluso?*	eh een-**kloo**-zoh
Where can I buy / find...?	*Dove posso comprare / trovare...?*	**doh**-vay **pos**-soh kohm-**prah**-ray / troh-**vah**-ray
I'd like / We'd like...	*Vorrei / Vorremmo...*	vor-**reh**ee / vor-**ray**-moh
...a room.	*...una camera.*	**oo**-nah **kah**-meh-rah
...a ticket to ___.	*...un biglietto per ___.*	oon beel-**yeht**-toh pehr
Is it possible?	*È possibile?*	eh poh-**see**-bee-lay
Where is...?	*Dov'è...?*	**doh**-veh
...the train station	*...la stazione*	lah staht-see**oh**-nay
...the bus station	*...la stazione degli autobus*	lah staht-see**oh**-nay **dayl**-yee **ow**-toh-boos
...tourist information	*...informazioni per turisti*	een-for-maht-see**oh**-nee pehr too-**ree**-stee
...the toilet	*...la toilette*	lah twah-**leht**-tay
men	*uomini, signori*	**woh**-mee-nee, seen-**yoh**-ree
women	*donne, signore*	**don**-nay, seen-**yoh**-ray
left / right	*sinistra / destra*	see-**nee**-strah / **dehs**-trah
straight	*sempre diritto*	**sehm**-pray dee-**ree**-toh
When do you open / close?	*A che ora aprite / chiudete?*	ah kay **oh**-rah ah-**pree**-tay / keeoo-**day**-tay
At what time?	*A che ora?*	ah kay **oh**-rah
Just a moment.	*Un momento.*	oon moh-**mayn**-toh
now / soon / later	*adesso / presto / tardi*	ah-**dehs**-soh / **prehs**-toh / **tar**-dee
today / tomorrow	*oggi / domani*	**oh**-jee / doh-**mah**-nee

In an Italian-speaking Restaurant

English	Italian	Pronunciation
I'd like...	Vorrei...	vor-**rehee**
We'd like...	Vorremmo...	vor-**ray**-moh
...to reserve...	...prenotare...	pray-noh-**tah**-ray
...a table for one / two.	...un tavolo per uno / due.	oon **tah**-voh-loh pehr **oo**-noh / **doo**-ay
Non-smoking.	Non fumare.	nohn foo-**mah**-ray
Is this seat free?	È libero questo posto?	eh **lee**-bay-roh **kwehs**-toh **poh**-stoh
The menu (in English), please.	Il menù (in inglese), per favore.	eel may-**noo** (een een-**glay**-zay) pehr fah-**voh**-ray
service (not) included	servizio (non) incluso	sehr-**veet**-seeoh (nohn) een-**kloo**-zoh
cover charge	pane e coperto	**pah**-nay ay koh-**pehr**-toh
to go	da portar via	dah **por**-tar **vee**-ah
with / without	con / senza	kohn / **sehn**-sah
and / or	e / o	ay / oh
menu (of the day)	menù (del giorno)	may-**noo** (dayl **jor**-noh)
specialty of the house	specialità della casa	spay-chah-lee-**tah dehl**-lah **kah**-zah
first course (pasta, soup)	primo piatto	**pree**-moh peeah-toh
main course (meat, fish)	secondo piatto	say-**kohn**-doh peeah-toh
side dishes	contorni	kohn-**tor**-nee
bread	pane	**pah**-nay
cheese	formaggio	for-**mah**-joh
sandwich	panino	pah-**nee**-noh
soup	minestra, zuppa	mee-**nehs**-trah, **tsoo**-pah
salad	insalata	een-sah-**lah**-tah
meat	carne	**kar**-nay
chicken	pollo	**poh**-loh
fish	pesce	**peh**-shay
seafood	frutti di mare	**froo**-tee dee **mah**-ray
fruit / vegetables	frutta / legumi	**froo**-tah / lay-**goo**-mee
dessert	dolci	**dohl**-chee
tap water	acqua del rubinetto	**ah**-kwah dayl roo-bee-**nay**-toh
mineral water	acqua minerale	**ah**-kwah mee-nay-**rah**-lay
milk	latte	**lah**-tay
(orange) juice	succo (d'arancia)	**soo**-koh (dah-**rahn**-chah)
coffee / tea	caffè / tè	kah-**feh** / teh
wine	vino	**vee**-noh
red / white	rosso / bianco	**roh**-soh / bee**ahn**-koh
glass / bottle	bicchiere / bottiglia	bee-kee**eay**-ray / boh-**teel**-yah
beer	birra	**bee**-rah
Cheers!	Cin cin!	cheen cheen
More. / Another.	Ancora un po.' / Un altro.	ahn-**koh**-rah oon poh / oon **ahl**-troh
The same.	Lo stesso.	loh **stehs**-soh
The bill, please.	Il conto, per favore.	eel **kohn**-toh pehr fah-**voh**-ray
tip	mancia	**mahn**-chah
Delicious!	Delizioso!	day-leet-seeoh-zoh

For more user-friendly Italian phrases, check out *Rick Steves' Italian Phrase Book & Dictionary* or *Rick Steves' French, Italian, and German Phrase Book*.

INDEX

Our website enhances this book and turns

Explore Europe

At ricksteves.com you can browse through thousands of articles, videos, photos and radio interviews, plus find a wealth of money-saving travel tips for planning your dream trip. And with our mobile-friendly website, you can easily access all this great travel information anywhere you go.

TV Shows

Preview the places you'll visit by watching entire half-hour episodes of Rick Steves' Europe (choose from all 100 shows) on-demand, for free.

Radio Interviews

Enjoy ready access to Rick's vast library of radio interviews covering travel

tips and cultural insights that relate specifically to your Europe travel plans.

Travel Forums

Learn, ask, share! Our online community of savvy travelers is a great resource for first-time travelers to Europe, as well as seasoned pros. You'll find forums on each country, plus travel tips and restaurant/hotel reviews. You can even ask one of our well-traveled staff to chime in with an opinion.

Travel News

Subscribe to our free Travel News e-newsletter, and get monthly updates from Rick on what's happening in Europe.

Rick's Free Travel App

Get your FREE **Rick Steves Audio Europe**™ app to enjoy…

- Dozens of self-guided tours of Europe's top museums, sights and historic walks

- Hundreds of tracks filled with cultural insights and sightseeing tips from Rick's radio interviews

- All organized into handy geographic playlists

- For iPhone, iPad, iPod Touch, Android

With Rick whispering in your ear, Europe gets even better.

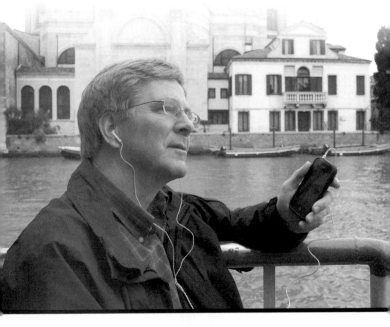

Find out more at ricksteves.com

Gear up for your next adventure at ricksteves.com

Light Luggage

Pack light and right with Rick Steves' affordable, custom-designed rolling carry-on bags, backpacks, day packs and shoulder bags.

Accessories

From packing cubes to moneybelts and beyond, Rick has personally selected the travel goodies that will help your trip go smoother.

Save time and energy

This guidebook is your independent-travel toolkit. But for all it delivers, it's still up to you to devote the time and energy it takes to manage the preparation and logistics that are essential for a happy trip. If that's a hassle, there's a solution.

Rick Steves Tours

A Rick Steves tour takes you to Europe's most interesting places with great

with minimum stress

guides and small groups of 28 or less. We follow Rick's favorite itineraries, ride in comfy buses, stay in family-run hotels, and bring you intimately close to the Europe you've traveled so far to see. Most importantly, we take away the logistical headaches so you can focus on the fun.

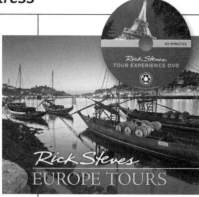

customers—along with us on 40 different itineraries, from Ireland to Italy to Istanbul. Is a Rick Steves tour the right fit for your travel dreams? Find out at ricksteves.com, where you can also get Rick's latest tour catalog and free Tour Experience DVD.

Join the fun

This year we'll take 18,000 free-spirited travelers— nearly half of them repeat

Europe is best experienced with happy travel partners. We hope you can join us.

See our itineraries at ricksteves.com

Rick Steves

Rick Steves guidebooks are published by Avalon Travel, a member of the Perseus Books Group.

Maximize your travel skills with a good guidebook.

TRAVEL CULTURE

Europe 101
European Christmas
Postcards from Europe
Travel as a Political Act

eBOOKS

Nearly all Rick Steves guides are available as ebooks. Check with your favorite bookseller.

RICK STEVES' EUROPE DVDs

12 New Shows 2015–2016
Austria & the Alps
The Complete Collection 2000-2016
Eastern Europe
England & Wales
European Christmas
European Travel Skills & Specials
France
Germany, BeNeLux & More
Greece, Turkey & Portugal
The Holy Land: Israelis & Palestinians Today
Iran
Ireland & Scotland
Italy's Cities
Italy's Countryside
Scandinavia
Spain
Travel Extras

PHRASE BOOKS & DICTIONARIES

French
French, Italian & German
German
Italian
Portuguese
Spanish

PLANNING MAPS

Britain, Ireland & London
Europe
France & Paris
Germany, Austria & Switzerland
Ireland
Italy
Spain & Portugal

Photo © Patricia Feaster

RickSteves.com 📷 ✖ @RickSteves

Rick Steves books are available at bookstores and through online booksellers.

Avalon Travel
a member of the Perseus Books Group
1700 Fourth Street
Berkeley, CA 94710

Printed in Canada by Friesens
First printing December 2015

ISBN 978-1-63121-205-5

For the latest on Rick's lectures, guidebooks, tours, public radio show, and public television series, contact Rick Steves' Europe, Inc., 130 Fourth Avenue North, Edmonds, WA
98020, tel. 425/771-8303, www.ricksteves.com, rick@ricksteves.com.

Rick Steves' Europe
Special Publications Manager: Risa Laib
Managing Editor: Jennifer Madison Davis
Editors: Glenn Eriksen, Tom Griffin, Katherine Gustafson, Suzanne Kotz, Cathy Lu,
    John Pierce, Carrie Shepherd
Editorial & Production Assistant: Jessica Shaw
Editorial Intern: Shirley Qiu
Researchers: Virginia Agostinelli, Ben Cameron, Trish Feaster, Cameron Hewitt,
    Suzanne Kotz
Contributor: Gene Openshaw
Maps & Graphics: David C. Hoerlein, Sandra Hundacker, Lauren Mills, Mary Rostad

Avalon Travel
Senior Editor and Series Manager: Madhu Prasher
Editor: Jamie Andrade
Associate Editor: Maggie Ryan
Copy Editors: Judith Brown and Suzie Nasol
Proofreader: Denise Silva
Indexer: Stephen Callahan
Production and Typesetting: Rue Flaherty, Tabitha Lahr
Cover Design: Kimberly Glyder Design
Maps & Graphics: Kat Bennett, Mike Morgenfeld

Photo Credits
Front Cover: The Galleria Vittorio Emanuele II, Milan © fazon1/istockphoto.com
Title Page: Bellagio © Anna-Mari West/123rf.com
Page 55: Street in front of Duomo Cathedral, Milan © Petunyia | Dreamstime.com
Additional Photography: Dominic Arizona Bonuccelli, Ben Cameron, Julie Coen,
Jennifer Hauseman, Cameron Hewitt, David C. Hoerlein, Gene Openshaw, Michael
Potter, Robyn Stencil, Rick Steves, Bruce VanDeventer, Laura VanDeventer, Les
Wahlstrom, Ian Watson, Tom Wallace, Wikimedia Commons (PD-Art/PD-US),
Deanna Woodruff (photos are used by permission and are the property of the original
copyright owners).